Exploring
America
in the **1950s**

Exploring
America
in the 1950s

Beneath the Formica

Grades 6–8

Molly Sandling &
Kimberley L. Chandler, Ph.D.

The College of William and Mary
School of Education
Center for Gifted Education
P.O. Box 8795
Williamsburg, VA 23187

Edited by Rachel Taliaferro

Production design by Raquel Trevino

ISBN-13: 978-1-61821-108-8

Prufrock Press Inc.
P.O. Box 8813
Waco, TX 76714-8813
Phone: (800) 998-2208
Fax: (800) 240-0333
http://www.prufrock.com

Contents

Acknowledgements

Thanks to Kimberly Turner Towne, who provided the background information about art referenced in this unit.

Thanks also to Pamela N. Harris, who acted as the editorial assistant for this unit.

Unit Overview

Introduction to the *Exploring America* Units

These humanities units focus on the ways in which the literature, art, and music of each decade from the 1950s through the 2000s reflect the history and events that were occurring in America at the time. These units are intended to stimulate student interest and creativity, to develop higher order thinking skills, and to promote interdisciplinary learning. The units could be used as a supplement to a social studies or language arts curriculum, or could be used as stand-alone materials in a gifted education program.

Introduction to *Exploring America in the 1950s: Beneath the Formica*

Exploring America in the 1950s: Beneath the Formica is about the difficulty in defining the identity of the U.S. during the Cold War as Americans struggled to balance being a world super-power with the corresponding anxiety about that influence and the weapons of mass destruction behind it. Topics included in the unit are:

- » music that reacted to the atomic bomb, which ended WWII and set the tone of the Cold War;
- » the tension between the fascination and fear of the new technology through science fiction literature;
- » songs and poetry that captured reactions to the Red Scare;

> » the change from an urban, industrial society to a suburban, service-based society and the ideals and culture of conformity that came with it;
> » reactions to the conformity of the 1950s as seen in the early Civil Rights movement;
> » music of the Civil Rights movement and the role of Elvis, as well as the reaction to it; and
> » rejection of conformity from the literature of the Beat generation and Abstract Expressionist art.

Standards Alignment

Social Studies

This unit includes activities that address the National Curriculum Standards for Social Studies (NCSS). Specifically, the activities relate to nine themes of the NCSS: Culture; Time, Continuity, and Change; People, Places, and Environments; Individual Development and Identity; Individuals, Groups, and Institutions; Power, Authority, and Governance; Production, Distribution, and Consumption; Science, Technology, and Society; and Global Connections, Civic Ideals, and Practices.

English Language Arts

This unit also includes activities that align to these College and Career Readiness Anchor Standards of the Common Core State Standards in English Language Arts (CCSS-ELA):

> » CCSS.ELA-Literacy.CCRA.R.1: Read closely to determine what the text says explicitly and to make logical inferences from it; cite specific textual evidence when writing or speaking to support conclusions drawn from the text.
> » CCSS.ELA-Literacy.CCRA.R.2: Determine central ideas or themes of a text and analyze their development; summarize the key supporting details and ideas.
> » CCSS.ELA-Literacy.CCRA.R.4: Interpret words and phrases as they are used in a text, including determining technical, connotative, and figurative meanings, and analyze how specific word choices shape meaning or tone.
> » CCSS.ELA-Literacy.CCRA.R.7: Integrate and evaluate content presented in diverse media and formats, including visually and quantitatively, as well as in words.
> » CCSS.ELA-Literacy.CCRA.R.9: Analyze how two or more texts address similar themes or topics in order to build knowledge or to compare the approaches the authors take.
> » CCSS.ELA-Literacy.CCRA.R.10: Read and comprehend complex literary and informational texts independently and proficiently.

Overarching Concept

The overarching concept for this unit is *identity*. This concept can help students to understand events, music, art, and literature during the 1950s. The unit explores the decade, giving students multiple opportunities to analyze events based on a developing understanding of how the idea of identity applies to specific situations. The conceptual approach also allows students the opportunity to make comparisons to other time periods, thus developing a deeper understanding of generalizations about identity and when they may or may not apply.

The first lesson in this unit introduces the concept of identity. Teachers may wish to conduct an activity based on Hilda Taba's (1962) Concept Development Model prior to teaching the first lesson. Students are asked to brainstorm examples of identity, categorize their examples, identify "nonexamples" of the concept, and make generalizations about the concept. The following generalizations about identity are incorporated into this unit of study:

» Identity changes with new ideas, experiences, conditions, or in response to other expressions of identity;

» Identity is created, either by a group or person or by outsiders, and self-created identities may be different from how others see one's self;

» There are multiple elements of identity and at different times, different elements have greater or lesser importance; and

» Although members of a group or society may have different individual identities, they still share particular elements of identity.

Identity is integrated throughout unit lessons and deepens students' understanding of social studies and a given historical period. Students examine the relationship of important ideas, abstractions, and issues through the application of the concept generalizations.

Curriculum Framework

Concept Goal

Goal 1: To understand the concept of identity in 1950s America. Students will be able to:

» describe how the American identity changed during the 1950s; and

» describe how changes in American identity in the 1950s are revealed in the music, art, and literature of the decade.

Process Goals

Goal 2: To develop skills in historical analysis and song and artwork interpretation. Students will be able to:

» define the context in which a song or piece of art was created and the implications of context for understanding the artifact;

» describe a writer's or artist's intent in producing a given song or piece of art based on understanding of text and context;

» consider short- and long-term consequences of a given document or artifact; and

» analyze the effects of given documents or artifacts on the interpretation of historical events.

Goal 3: To develop analytical and interpretive skills in literature. Students will be able to:

» describe what a selected literary passage means;

» cite similarities and differences in meaning among selected works of literature; and

» make inferences based on information in given passages.

Content Goal

Goal 4: To develop an understanding of historical events occurring in the United States during the 1950s. Students will be able to:

» describe major historical events during the 1950s that affected the American identity; and

» describe music, art, and literature of the 1950s that reflected the American identity.

Assessing Student Learning

For formative assessments, teachers should evaluate student progress based on the quality of individual products and achievement toward the goals of the unit. Question responses should be assessed based on demonstration of insight and ability to use text to support inferences. Writing activities should be assessed based on understanding of the social studies content, and may also be assessed for clarity and insight as desired. Oral presentations of completed work should be assessed based on coherence, content, and clarity of the presentation. Teachers may provide rubrics for students related to the required assignments or work with students to develop rubrics for assessment.

The culminating project for the unit, the "The Ed Sullivan Show Project," will provide a comprehensive, summative assessment that evaluates student learning about all four unit goals. Based on their study of the 1950s, students are to plan the schedule for one night of The Ed Sullivan Show, including the acts and personalities that will appear and why these are important figures to include in the show's lineup. This is an opportunity for students to expand their study beyond the figures covered in the unit.

Teaching Resources

Recommended History Textbooks

Appleby, J. (2010). *American vision*. New York, NY: Glencoe/McGraw Hill.

Cayton, A. R. L., Perry, E. I., Reed, L., & Winkler, A. M. (2002). *Pathways to the present*. Upper Saddle River, NJ: Pearson Prentice Hall.

Davidson, J. W., Stoff, M. B., & Viola, H. J. (2002). *The American nation*. Upper Saddle River, NJ: Pearson Prentice Hall.

Kennedy, D. M., & Cohen, L. (2012). *American pageant*. Boston, MA: Cengage Learning.

Recommended Websites

» *The Ed Sullivan Show* website: http://www.edsullivan.com

» Internet Archive Movie Archive: http://archive.org/details/movies

» Library of Congress Song and Poetry Analysis Tools: http://www.loc.gov/teachers/lyrical/tools

» Rock and Roll Hall of Fame Education Resources: http://www.rockhall.com/education

» Smithsonian Folkways: http://www.folkways.si.edu

Implementation Guide

This guide assists the teacher in implementing this unit in his or her classroom. It also includes background information about the instructional models utilized throughout the unit.

Guidelines

The following pages offer some general suggestions to help the teacher implement the unit effectively.

Support for Teachers Implementing the Unit

It is important for teachers implementing this unit to read it in depth before beginning instruction. Conferences and training workshops sponsored through the Center for Gifted Education (CFGE) can help teachers understand the core components of the unit and provide informal tips for teaching it. Customized professional development, including comprehensive curriculum planning for incorporating this humanities series, is also available. Please contact the CFGE at cfgepd@wm.edu for information about professional development options.

Suggested Grade Levels

Exploring America in the 1950s was designed for use with high-ability students in grades 6–8. Although the unit was developed for middle school students, some components may work well with students at other grade levels. Caution should be exercised when using the materials with elementary-aged students, however, as some of the music and literature contains mature themes.

How to Incorporate the Unit Within the Existing Social Studies Curriculum

This unit is intended to represent 5–8 weeks of instruction in social studies for high-ability learners. The unit may be taught as core content, or it may be used as a supplement to the core curriculum. The unit is also appropriate for use in a seminar setting.

Implementation Time

In this unit, a lesson is defined as at least two 2-hour sessions. A minimum of 40 instructional hours should be allocated for teaching the entire unit. Teachers are encouraged to extend the amount of time spent on the various topics included in the book based on available time and student interest.

Materials

Availability of materials. Given that this unit focuses on the 1950s decade, the materials are contemporary in nature and have not yet become part of the public domain. In most cases, it is suggested that teachers make use of Internet resources whenever possible rather than purchasing the materials cited. Both Prufrock Press and the Center for Gifted Education have developed websites that include a list of resources and their respective URLs: http://www.prufrock.com/Assets/ClientPages/exploring1950.aspx and http://education.wm.edu/centers/cfge/1950s. Because URLs tend to change, these websites will be updated periodically.

Potentially controversial materials. This unit focuses on the trends and issues in 1950s America. Some topics being discussed and some of the materials being used may be controversial to some students and parents. It is crucial that teachers preview all materials prior to teaching the unit and determine what is appropriate for their own schools and classrooms.

Teachers should always read the literature selections or listen to the musical selections before assigning them to students and be aware of what the school and/or district policy is on the use of materials that may be deemed controversial. Although many gifted readers are able to read books at a significantly higher Lexile level than what other children their age are reading, content that is targeted at older audiences may not be appropriate for them.

Text/Song/Artwork

☐ Made original, insightful contribution(s) to discussion?

☐ Extended or elaborated on a classmate's ideas?

☐ Used evidence from the text or another student's comments to support ideas?

☐ Synthesized information from discussion in a meaningful way?

☐ Posed questions that enhanced the discussion and led to more in-depth understanding?

Student comments: _____

_____

_____

Teacher comments: _____

_____

_____

Figure 1. Participation Checklist. Adapted from Center for Gifted Education (2011).

Assessment

This unit includes both formative and summative assessments, which are found at the end of each lesson plan. Because discussion plays a prominent role in the students' learning in this unit, teachers may want to consider teaching students a specific process for the discussion elements and develop tools for assessing student participation. The Socratic Seminar is one method for organizing discussions. (See http://socraticseminars.com/socratic-seminars/ or http://www.readwritethink.org/professional-development/strategy-guides/socratic-seminars-30600.html for additional information.) Or, the teacher may want to design a checklist, such as the one in Figure 1, to give to students to keep track of their contributions during discussions. The students can check off the criteria as they meet them. Using this checklist, the student and teacher can monitor the student's participation in various discussions.

Teaching Models

There are five teaching models that are used in the unit to facilitate student achievement toward the unit objectives. Teachers should familiarize themselves with these models before beginning the unit.

The models are designed to promote discussions in various settings. The teacher should determine the best way of organizing students for discussion in order to facilitate student understanding and appreciation for the variety of answers that are given. These teaching models also provide students with the opportunity to support their responses with evidence from the literature or other resources. Multiple perspectives can be shared and encouraged through appropriate use of the models. The models also may be used to prepare students for a discussion in another content area or about a current event. Students can complete the models in a whole group, in small groups, or individually before or as they engage in a discussion. Varying the group size and group composition will provide students with many perspectives for consideration. For more information, see Center for Gifted Education (2011).

The models are listed below and described in the pages that follow.

1. Identity Chart
2. Literature Analysis Model
3. Primary Source Document Analysis Model
4. Music Analysis Model
5. Art Analysis Model

Identity Chart

The Identity Chart (see Figure 2) allows students to consider the concept of identity as they study the events of the mid-20th century and examine the effect of those events on the American identity. Some scholars (Huntington, 2004; Smith, 2010) have defined the elements that comprise identity; for purposes of this unit, these include:

»   time and place,
»   history and myths,
»   culture and traditions,
»   race and ethnicity,
»   civic identity,
»   international role, and
»   economy.

Prior to the first lesson, you may have students develop a list of the elements that they believe are part of the American identity, and then compare it to the one listed here. Have students determine the definition of each element and give examples.

Tell students that in this unit, they will be examining the American identity in the 1950s, trying to get a better understanding of why Americans interacted as they did. Explain that identity is important because it shapes our actions and interactions with others. Have students answer the following questions on their own, then debrief in the large group:

»   Do all of the elements of identity that we listed affect your actions equally at all times? Explain your answer.
»   Sometimes various elements of identity are emphasized more than others. What are some examples? Why does this happen?
»   When is each of these elements most important? Least important? Why?
»   Which elements are most influential on your actions when you are at school? When you go on vacation? When you meet someone new? When you have to make an important decision? Why?

Explain that the questions and responses just discussed address individual (personal) identity. Have students answer the following questions:

»   What other types of identity are there?
»   How can a group's identity be different from an individual's identity within that group?

HANDOUT

Identity Chart

Identity	
	Time and Place
	Culture and Traditions
	History and Myths
	International Role
	Economy
	Civic Identity
	Race/Ethnicity

Figure 2. Identity Chart.

This discussion serves as the initial one regarding identity, specifically the American identity in the 1950s. Other unit activities will reinforce this concept. Teachers should revisit the identity generalizations regularly throughout the unit and make specific connections to the 1950s.

Literature Analysis Model

The Literature Analysis Model (see Figure 3) encourages students to consider seven aspects of a selection they are reading: key words, tone, mood, imagery, symbolism, key ideas, and the structure of writing (Center for Gifted Education, 2011; McKeague, 2009; National Governors Association Center for Best Practices & Council of Chief State School Officers, 2010). After reading a selection, this model helps students to organize their initial responses and provides them with a basis for discussing the piece in small or large groups. Whenever possible, students should be allowed to underline and make notes as they read the material. After marking the text, they can organize their notes into the model.

Suggested questions for completing and discussing the model are:

HANDOUT

Literature Analysis Model

Chosen or assigned text:	
Key words:	
Important ideas:	
Tone:	
Mood:	
Imagery:	
Symbolism:	
Structure of writing:	

Figure 3. Literature Analysis Model.

1. **Key words:** What words are important for understanding the selection? Which words did the author use for emphasis?
2. **Important ideas:** What is the main idea of the selection? What are other important ideas in the selection?
3. **Tone:** What is the attitude or what are the feelings of the author toward the subject of the selection? What words does the author use to indicate tone?
4. **Mood:** What emotions do you feel when reading the selection? How do the setting, images, objects, and details contribute to the mood?
5. **Imagery:** What are examples of the descriptive language that is used to create sensory impressions in the selection?
6. **Symbolism:** What symbols are used to represent other things?
7. **Structure of writing:** What are some important characteristics of the way this piece is written? How do the parts of this selection fit together and relate to each other? How do structural elements contribute to the meaning of the piece?

After students have completed their Literature Analysis Models individually, they should compare their answers in small groups. These small groups may compile a composite model that includes the ideas of all members. Following the small-group work, teachers have several options for using the models. For instance, they may ask each group to report to the class, they may ask groups to post their composite models, or they may develop a new Literature Analysis Model with the class based on the small-group work. It is important for teachers to hold a whole-group discussion as the final aspect of implementing this model as a teaching-learning device. Teachers are also encouraged to display the selection on a document camera or overhead projector as it is discussed and make appropriate annotations. The teacher should record ideas, underline words listed, and call attention to student responses visually. The teacher should conclude the discussion by asking open-ended follow-up questions. For more information about analyzing literature, see Center for Gifted Education (2011).

Primary Source Document Analysis Model

The Primary Source Document Analysis Model has been developed as a way to teach students:

- » how to interpret a historical document,
- » how to pose questions to ask about it, and
- » how to examine information in the document critically.

The handout (see Figure 4) is designed to assist students as they work through this Primary Source Document Analysis Model. The information that follows includes additional questions and ideas meant to facilitate use of the model. This questions in this model assume the author had an agenda or plan about a specific issue. Thus, it may not be appropriate for use with all primary source documents. For more information about primary sources, see Center for Gifted Education (2007) and Library of Congress (n.d.).

What is the title of the document? Why was it given this title? Students should write the title of the document in this space. The discussion should include probing of why the document was given this title.

What is your reaction to the document? The student will engage with the document and use prior knowledge to make some initial observations and comments. To do that, have students read the document and answer the questions based on their first impressions. You could also revisit the questions on this part of the model after a more thorough analysis of the document has been completed.

When was the document written? Why was it written? The student will focus on the context of the document, as well as its purpose. In order to do that, students must consider the following:

1. Students need to understand the beliefs, norms, and values—the culture—of the period in which the document was developed.
2. Students also need to think about other relevant events and prevalent opinions concerning this issue that were occurring at the time the document was created.
3. Students need to consider the *context*. Additional questions to explore the context could include:
   - ○ Who had control of the situation? Who wanted control, but didn't have it?

HANDOUT

Primary Source Document Analysis Model

Document: _____

What is the title of the document? Why was it given this title?

Title:
Why do you think it was given this title?
Which words in the title are especially important? Why?

What is your reaction to the document?

What is the first thing about this document that draws your attention?
What is in the document that surprises you, or that you didn't expect?
What are some of the powerful ideas expressed in the document?
What feelings does the primary source cause in you?
What questions does it raise for you?

When was the document written? Why was it written?

Who is the author(s)?
When was the document written?
What do you know about the culture of the time period in which the document was written?
What were the important events occurring at the time the document was written?
What was the author's purpose in writing this document?
Who is the intended audience?
What biases do you see in the author's text?

What are the important ideas in this document?

What problems or events does the document address?
What is the author's main point or argument?
What actions or outcomes does the author expect? From whom?
How do you think this author would define *American identity*? What elements of the American identity does the author see as being threatened or cultivated? Why?

What is your evaluation of this document?

Is this document authentic? How do you know?
Is this author a reliable source for addressing this issue/problem?
How representative is this document of the views of the people at this time in history?
How does this document compare with others of the same time period?
What could have been the possible consequences of this document?
What actually happened as a result of this document? Discuss the long-term, short-term, and unintended consequences.
What interpretation of this historical period does this document provide?
How does this document contribute to your understanding of the American identity during this time period?

Figure 4. Primary Source Document Analysis Model.

   ○ Who and what were important to people at this time?

   ○ What did people at this time hope for or value?

   ○ Was this issue a new one, an ongoing one, one that was being debated frequently at the time, or one in which few people were interested?

   ○ What were the major events occurring at the time the document was written?

   ○ What were the societal trends occurring at the time this document was written?

4. Once students have determined the context for the document, the next step is to focus on the *purpose* of the document. Additional questions to explore the purpose include:

   ○ Why did the author write this?

   ○ Did a specific event or opinion of the time inspire this document? If so, what was it?

   ○ Did the author have a personal experience that led him or her to write this?

   ○ Did someone require or ask the author to write the document?

   ○ How does the purpose affect the content of the document?

5. Connected to purpose is the *audience*. The same author may write differently for specific groups of people. The primary audience can affect the interpretation of the document.

   ○ For whom was the document created?

   ○ How did the proposed audience affect the content of the document?

What are the important ideas in this document? Once students understand the context and purpose of the document, they will analyze what the document means. Additional questions for probing student understanding of the document's *important ideas* could include:

 » What assumptions/values/feelings are reflected in the document?

 » What is the author's opinion about the issue?

 » Is the author empathetic about the situation, or critical of it?

 » Is the author an insider or outsider relative to the issue? Is the author personally involved with the issue or is he or she an observer?

Finally, because the author had a purpose for writing the document, he or she must expect something to happen as a result. These questions can provide additional prompting of student understanding of the *possible results*:

 » Who does the author expect to take action in this situation?

 » Does the author expect people to change their opinions, to take a specific action, or to consider a new idea?

What is your evaluation of this document? Students will evaluate the document to identify its effectiveness, both for those in the past and for us in the present.

1. The first set of questions focuses on the *authenticity* and *reliability* of a source to help students decide whether or not a document is what it claims or appears to be.

   ○ Authenticity relates to whether the document is real, and not altered or an imitation. Historical documents often have passed through many hands; in doing so, editors or translators may have altered the words or the meaning of the document accidentally or intentionally to reflect their own agendas (Center for Gifted Education, 2007).

○ Reliability relates to the author's qualifications for addressing a given issue or event. In order to write something reliable, authors need to have adequate information and experience with the topic being discussed (Center for Gifted Education, 2007).

Additional questions for discussing the authenticity and reliability of a source are:
○ Could the document have been fabricated, edited, or mistranslated?
○ What evidence do you need to verify the accuracy of the document?
○ What evidence do you have to show that the document was altered at a later time?
○ How reliable is this author?
○ Is the author an authority on this issue, or does he or she have sufficient knowledge to write about it?

2. The second set of questions focuses on how *representative* a document is of views of the time. This requires students to identify the prevalence of the stated ideas in society at the time the document was written.
   ○ Would many, some, or few people have agreed with the ideas stated in this document?
   ○ How do the ideas in this document relate to the context of the period in which it was written?
   ○ How does this document compare with others from the same period? Are there other documents from the time that express similar ideas? Different ideas?
   ○ What other information might you need to confirm this?

3. The third set of questions relates to considering the *consequences* of a document. First, students must consider the possible outcomes and then the actual ones. By considering the possible outcomes, students can see that multiple options for outcomes existed.
   ○ What could the possible consequences of this document have been?
   ○ What might happen if the author's plans were implemented?
   ○ What could the reaction to the author be when people read this?
   ○ How might this document affect or change public opinions?
   ○ What actually happened as a result of this document?
   ○ How did this document affect people's lives or events at the time (short-term effects)?
   ○ How did the document affect people at other times in the past, or how does it affect us today (long-term effects)?
   ○ What were the unintended consequences of this document?

4. The fourth set of questions helps students to determine *how the interpretation informs* the reader about the historical period:
   ○ What new interpretation of the historical period does this document provide for the reader?
   ○ How does the document provide an interpretation about the historical period that is not provided through other materials of the time?
   ○ How does this interpretation inform us about the American identity during this time period?

○ The implementation of this model may be handled similarly to the way in which discussions are held using the Literature Analysis Model: After students have completed their Primary Source Document Analysis Models individually, they should compare their answers in small groups. These small groups may compile a composite model that includes the ideas of all members. Following the small-group work, teachers have several options for using the models, including developing a composite, whole-class model, or posting group models and discussing them. It is important for teachers to hold a group discussion as the final aspect of implementing this model as a teaching-learning device. Teachers are also encouraged to display the selection on a document camera or overhead projector as it is discussed and make appropriate annotations. The teacher should record ideas, underline words listed, and call attention to student responses visually. The teacher should conclude the discussion by asking open-ended follow-up questions.

Music Analysis Model

The Music Analysis Model (see Figure 5) has been developed as a means for teaching students:

» how to interpret lyrics from a song,
» how to pose questions to ask about it, and
» how to examine information in the song critically.

When working with specific songs, encourage students to think critically about both the *lyrics* and *orchestration*, keeping the elements of identity in mind. The Music Analysis Model uses the same key questions as the Primary Source Document Analysis Model, but with wording specifically related to songs:

» What is the title of the song? Why was it given this title?
» What is your reaction to the song?
» When was the song written? Why was it written?
» What are the important ideas in this song?
» What is your evaluation of this song?

As such, many of the same questions listed above for the Primary Source Document Analysis Model may be used for additional probing into student understanding. For additional suggestions about the implementation of this model, please see the note regarding how to manage class discussions after students have completed the Primary Source Document Analysis Model.

Art Analysis Model

The Art Analysis Model (see Figure 6) has been developed as a means for teaching students:

» how to interpret a piece of artwork,
» how to pose questions to ask about it, and
» how to examine the piece of artwork critically.

HANDOUT

Music Analysis Model

Song Title:_____

What is the title of the song? Why was it given this title?

Title:
Why do you think it was given this title?
Which words in the title are especially important? Why?

What is your reaction to the song?

What is the first thing about this song that draws your attention?
What is in the song that surprises you, or that you didn't expect?
What are some of the powerful ideas expressed in the song?
What feelings does the song cause in you?
What questions does it raise for you?

When was the song written? Why was it written?

Who is the songwriter(s)?
When was the song written?
What is the song's purpose? To entertain? To dance to? To critique something?
What were the important events occurring at the time the song was written?
Who is the intended audience?
What biases do you see in the author's lyrics?

What are the important ideas in this song?

Lyrics	Music/Accompaniment
What is the subject of the song? Summarize the song.	Describe the music or melody of this song. Is it fast-paced or slow? Does it have low notes or high notes? Is it melodic or does it have lots of percussion?
What are the main points of the song? What is the song saying about the subject?	What feelings do you get from the music? Why?
What mood/values/feelings does the singer have about the topic?	How does the tone or mood of the music fit with the lyrics? Why might this be?

What is your evaluation of this song?

What new or different interpretation of this historical period does this song provide?
What does this song portray about American identity or how Americans felt at the time?

Figure 5. Music Analysis Model.

HANDOUT

Art Analysis Model

Artist: _____

Artwork/Image: _____

What is the title of the artwork? Why was it given this title?

Title:
Why do you think it was given this title?
Which words in the title are especially important? Why?
What does the title reveal about the artwork?

What do you see in the artwork?

What objects, shapes, or people do you see?
What colors does the artist use? Why?
Are the images in the work realistic or abstract?
What materials does the artist use? Why?

What is your reaction to the image?

What is the first thing about this image that draws your attention?
What is in the image that surprises you, or that you didn't expect?
What are some of the powerful ideas expressed in the image?
What feelings does the image cause in you?
What questions does it raise for you?

When was the image produced? Why was it produced?

Who is the artist?
When was the artwork produced?
What were the important events occurring at the time the artwork was produced?
What was the author's purpose in producing this artwork?
Who is the intended audience?

What are the important ideas in this artwork?

What assumptions/values/feelings are reflected in the artwork?
What are the artist's views about the issue(s)?

What is your evaluation of this artwork?

What new or different interpretation of this historical period does this artwork provide?
What does this artwork portray about American identity or how Americans felt at the time?

Figure 6. Art Analysis Model.

When working with specific pieces of art, encourage students to think critically about both the *image* and the *materials*, keeping the elements of identity in mind. The Art Analysis Model uses many of the same key questions as the Primary Source Document Analysis Model, but with wording specifically related to artwork:

» What is the title of the artwork? Why was it given this title?
» What do you see in the artwork?
» What is your reaction to the image?
» When was the image produced? Why was it produced?
» What are the important ideas in this artwork?
» What is your evaluation of this artwork?

For additional suggestions about the implementation of this model, please see the note regarding how to manage class discussions after students have completed the Primary Source Document Analysis Model.

Summary: Teaching Models

The five teaching models that are included in this unit are essential for facilitating discussions and attaining unit objectives. Teachers should familiarize themselves with these models before beginning the unit and attempt to use them with fidelity. It is important that they use the models repeatedly, as students need practice interacting with the models' components and understanding the questions.

LESSON 1

From World War to Cold War

Alignment of Unit Goals

> » Goal 1: To understand the concept of identity in 1950s America.
> » Goal 2: To develop skills in historical analysis and song and artwork interpretation.
> » Goal 3: To develop analytical and interpretive skills in literature.
> » Goal 4: To develop an understanding of historical events occurring in the United States during the 1950s.

Unit Objectives

> » To describe how changes in American identity in the 1950s are revealed in the music, art, and literature of the decade;
> » To define the context in which a song or piece of art was produced and the implications of context for understanding the artifact;
> » To describe what a selected literary passage means; and
> » To describe music, art, and literature of the 1950s that reflected the American identity.

Resources for Unit Implementation

» **Handout 1.1:** Identity Chart

» **Handout 1.2:** Identity Generalizations

» **Handout 1.3:** Music Analysis Model

» **Handout 1.4:** Confronting the Atomic Bomb

» **Handout 1.5:** Unit Project

» **Listen:** "Atom and Evil" by Golden Gate Quartet (1947). The song is available online at http://www.youtube.com/watch?v=BjIF646bA.

» **Listen:** "Old Man Atom" (Partlow, 1950) by The Sons of the Pioneers. The song is available online at http://www.youtube.com/watch?v=DrGSIcfJ-Tc.

» **Listen:** "Great Atomic Power" (Louvin, Louvin, & Bain, 1952) by The Louvin Brothers. The song is available online at http://www.youtube.com/watch?v=G9xB7usNSPo.

» **Read:** "If I Forget Thee, O Earth" by Arthur C. Clarke (1953). An online version is available at http://hermiene.net/short-stories/if_i_forget_thee.html.

» **Watch:** "Duck and Cover: Bert the Turtle Civil Defense Film" (United States Federal Civil Defense Administration [USFCDA], 1951). The video is available on YouTube at http://www.youtube.com/watch?v=IKqXu-5jw60.

» **Listen:** "When They Drop the Atomic Bomb" by Jackie Doll (1951) and His Pickled Peppers. The song is available online at http://www.youtube.com/watch?v=W7V4tOdboWA.

» **Watch:** Video clips of *The Ed Sullivan Show*. Many clips are available on YouTube.

Key Terms

» *Identity*: the characteristics by which a person or thing is recognized

Learning Experiences

1. Explain to students that following World War II, the United States went through economic, political, and cultural changes that altered people's perceptions of themselves, their country, and their role in the world. In order to understand how these changes affected the average American, students will examine the music, literature, and art that was produced and consumed in the U.S. at the time. To see the changes, they first need to review what was going on in America at the time and how Americans viewed themselves and their country at the end of World War II.

2. Tell students that as they study the 1950s, they will focus on American identity, how it changed throughout the last half of the 20th century, and how those changes are revealed in the music, art, and literature of the time. In a whole group, brainstorm together responses to the following questions and display student responses to examine them. **Ask:** What is identity? What are the various aspects or parts of someone's identity? Why is a person's identity important? What role does a person's identity play in how he or she acts or what he or she does? Discuss student responses as a class.

3. Distribute the Identity Chart (Handout 1.1) to students and explain to them that some scholars have developed categories of elements that define identity, such as family, race, ethnicity, individuality, beliefs, values, nationality, social class, time, and place. Use this to try to define American identity in 1944. This should serve to review material you have been covering in class. As a whole group, work through the pieces of the chart. **Ask:**

   a. **Time and place:** What do we put in those boxes? What is our nationality? What are our national symbols and sources of pride? What shared symbols or traditions represent American identity and are seen as meaningful by most Americans?

   b. **History and myths:** What is the shared background or heritage of the U.S.? What recent events or experiences shape American views?

   c. **Culture and traditions:** What is the American idea of family at this time? What are American values in 1944?

   d. **Race and ethnicity:** What is the status of the races in 1944? What is the role of ethnicity in 1944?

   e. **Civic identity:** What is the role of the citizen in America? What are our rights and duties as citizens?

   f. **International role:** What beliefs does America have about itself and others in the world?

   g. **Economy:** What does the U.S. produce and how does the U.S. generate revenue? What types of jobs do most people have? What is the status of the U.S. economy?

4. Explain to students that they will look at how the events and experiences of the 1950s altered American identity by using a set of generalizations. Distribute the Identity Generalizations sheet (Handout 1.2) to students and explain that the class will work through it together using Handout 1.1.

   a. The first generalization is "*Identity changes with new ideas, experiences, and conditions, or in response to other expressions of identity.*" **Ask:** What new ideas, experiences, or conditions arose out of the war? Have students hypothesize about how these might have affected American identity.

   b. The second generalization is "*Identity is created, either by a group or person or by outsiders, and self-created identities may be different from how others see one's self.*" **Ask:** How did America see itself in the world? How did the Soviet Union see America? Likewise, how did Germany and Japan see America? How did these different views shape America's role in the world?

   c. The third generalization is "*There are multiple elements of identity and at different times, different elements have greater or lesser importance.*" **Ask:** Which elements of identity were most significant in 1944? How might these priorities have shifted after the war?

    d.   The fourth generalization is *"Although members of a group or society may have different individual identities, they still share particular elements of identity."* **Ask:** Despite individual differences, which elements of identity did all Americans have in common?

5.   Explain to students that they will use these generalizations on identity and the concept of identity as they study the events of the late 20th century and examine the effect of those events on American identity. In this lesson, they will start by looking at the effect of new technologies on America. In 1945, the United States dropped two atomic bombs on Japan. The United States was the only country to use this incredibly destructive new weapon against another country. Give students a Music Analysis Model (Handout 1.3) and play for students the songs "Atom and Evil" by Golden Gate Quartet (1947), "Old Man Atom" (Partlow, 1950) by The Sons of the Pioneers, and "Great Atomic Power" (Louvin, Louvin, & Bain, 1952) by The Louvin Brothers. Give students a Confronting the Atomic Bomb sheet (Handout 1.4). **Ask:** How do the songs view the atomic bomb? What do the songs say the bomb is going to do? Based on the songs, how do you think the songwriters view the future? What images and allusions do the artists use? Why do they use these images? What do these songs tell us about the popular mindset regarding the new atomic bomb?

6.   Have students read "If I Forget Thee, O Earth" by Arthur C. Clarke (1953). **Ask:** What is happening in the story? What is the Colony? Where is it? Why? What are Marvin and his father going to see? What is the state of Earth? Why? How does Marvin feel about Earth? What are Marvin's hopes for Earth? What does this tell us about how Arthur C. Clarke views the atomic bomb? What is the message or meaning of the story?

7.   Explain to students that one of the reasons such fear of nuclear weapons existed was due to the tensions of the Cold War. Once the Soviet Union developed its own atomic and nuclear weapons, Americans became concerned about a possible nuclear attack on the U.S. Watch the "Duck and Cover: Bert the Turtle Civil Defense Film" (USFCDA, 1951). **Ask:** According to this public service announcement, how likely is a Soviet nuclear attack on the U.S.? If you were young, how might this make you feel? Based on the songs, story, and video, briefly describe what you think it was like to be someone living during the Cold War. What thoughts, feelings, fears, and hopes might people have had? What was the effect of this political tension on everyday people?

8.   Discuss the Korean War with students using any of the recommended history textbooks. Play the song "When They Drop the Atomic Bomb" (Doll, 1951) by Jackie Doll and his Pickled Peppers. **Ask:** How does this song view atomic technology? How is this song's view different from that of the other three? Why is this? How might the conflict in Korea explain the change in views? This song was written in 1951, right between "Old Man Atom" and "Great Atomic Power." What do these very different attitudes being expressed at the same time tell us about how the U.S. feels about its role in the world? What do these attitudes reveal about the American view of the atomic bomb?

9.   Summarize the songs and story with students by either having students formulate answers in small groups and report to the whole class, or by discussing as a whole class. **Ask:** Based on the story and the songs, how is American identity changing with the new experiences and conditions presented by the atomic bomb? Were Americans as confident about the U.S.'s role in the world in 1951 as they were in 1944? This period of history

is often referred to as "The Age of Anxiety." Based on the songs and story, is this an appropriate title? Why or why not?

10. Assign students the unit project, to be due at the end of the study of the 1950s. Give students a Unit Project sheet (Handout 1.5). Explain that one of the popular shows of the 1950s was *The Ed Sullivan Show*. This show was a variety show that had different celebrities and acts on every week and was notable for showcasing major music acts as well as important figures of the time. *The Ed Sullivan Show* started and ended each episode with a major up-and-coming musical group or artist such as Elvis Presley, The Beatles, The Rolling Stones, The Supremes, and others. The middle of the show included a wide variety of features ranging from comedy acts to interviews with political figures like Fidel Castro. Based on their study of the 1950s, students are to plan the schedule for one night of *The Ed Sullivan Show*, including the acts and personalities that will appear and why these are important figures to include in the show's lineup. This is an opportunity for students to expand their study beyond the figures covered in the unit. Encourage students to research people or events not covered and to talk with parents, grandparents, relatives, or neighbors who experienced the 1950s for ideas of public figures they can include in their project. The students have some freedom in the format and type of individuals that they include, but their choices should reflect important cultural and social trends of the 1950s. The teacher could assign some figures that need to be covered or allow students complete freedom of choice.

Assessing Student Learning

- » Identity Chart
- » Music Analysis Model
- » Discussions

Extending Student Learning

The following are optional activities for extending student learning in this lesson:
- » Along with a partner, have a student script and perform a radio broadcast from the 1950s. They should include the disc jockey's dialogue and specific song and artist information. **Ask:** What might the first radio broadcasts of rock and roll music have sounded like? How might rock and roll have gotten its name?
- » Have the student select the 10 most important events that occurred during the 1950s and create a timeline using PowerPoint or Prezi. The presentation should include a rationale for why each event was selected. (This activity could be presented at the conclusion of the unit.)

Name:_____ Date:_____

HANDOUT 1.1
Identity Chart

Directions: Complete each box with the elements that define each category of identity.

Identity	
	Time and Place
	Culture and Traditions
	History and Myths
	International Role
	Economy
	Civic Identity
	Race/Ethnicity

Name:_____ Date: _____

HANDOUT 1.2
Identity Generalizations

Directions: Use your completed Identity Chart to explain how each generalization below defines the start of the 1950s.

Identity changes with new ideas, experiences, and conditions, or in response to other expressions of identity.
Identity is created, either by a group or person or by outsiders, and self-created identities may be different from how others see one's self.
There are multiple elements of identity and at different times, different elements have greater or lesser importance.
Although members of a group or society may have different individual identities, they still share particular elements of identity.

Name:_____ Date: _____

HANDOUT 1.3
Music Analysis Model

Directions: Complete the boxes below after listening to the assigned songs.

Song Title:_____

What is the title of the song? Why was it given this title?

Title:
Why do you think it was given this title?
Which words in the title are especially important? Why?

What is your reaction to the song?

What is the first thing about this song that draws your attention?
What is in the song that surprises you, or that you didn't expect?
What are some of the powerful ideas expressed in the song?
What feelings does the song cause in you?
What questions does it raise for you?

Name:_____ Date:_____

When was the song written? Why was it written?

Who is the songwriter(s)?	
When was the song written?	
What is the song's purpose? To entertain? To dance to? To critique something?	
What were the important events occurring at the time the song was written?	
Who is the intended audience?	
What biases do you see in the author's lyrics?	

What are the important ideas in this song?

Lyrics	Music/Accompaniment
What is the subject of the song? Summarize the song.	Describe the music or melody of this song. Is it fast-paced or slow? Does it have low notes or high notes? Is it melodic or does it have lots of percussion?
What are the main points of the song? What is the song saying about the subject?	What feelings do you get from the music? Why?
What mood/values/feelings does the singer have about the topic?	How does the tone or mood of the music fit with the lyrics? Why might this be?

What is your evaluation of this song?

What new or different interpretation of this historical period does this song provide?
What does this song portray about American identity or how Americans felt at the time?

HANDOUT 1.4
Confronting the Atomic Bomb

Listen: "Atom and Evil" by the Golden Gate Quartet, "Old Man Atom" by The Sons of the Pioneers, and "Great Atomic Power" by The Louvin Brothers.

1. How do the songs portray the atomic bomb? What do the songs say the bomb is going to do?

2. How do the songs portray the future?

3. What images and allusions do the songs use? Why?

4. What do these songs tell us about the popular mindset about the new atomic bomb in the 1950s?

Read: "If I Forget Thee, O Earth" by Arthur C. Clarke.

1. What is the Colony and how did the people get there?

Handout 1.4: Confronting the Atomic Bomb, continued

2. What has happened to Earth? Why? What is the state of Earth?

3. How does this story feel about atomic weapons and what is its message?

Watch: "Duck and Cover: Bert the Turtle Civil Defense Film"
1. According to this film, how likely is a Soviet nuclear attack on the U.S.?

2. If you were young, how might this film make you feel?

Based on the songs, story, and video, briefly describe what you think it was like to be someone living during the Cold War. What thoughts, feelings, fears, and hopes might these people have had? What was the effect of the political tension surrounding the atomic bomb and the Cold War on everyday people?

HANDOUT 1.5
Unit Project

The Ed Sullivan Show

One of the popular shows of the 1950s was *The Ed Sullivan Show*. This show was a variety show (a show consisting of a series of short, unrelated performances) that had many different celebrities and acts on every week. *The Ed Sullivan Show* was notable for showcasing major music acts as well as the Hollywood/Broadway/sports figures of the time. Based on your study of the 1950s, you are to plan the schedule for one night of *The Ed Sullivan Show*, including which acts and personalities will appear and why these are important figures to include in the show's line up. You must pick and justify who will appear on your show to demonstrate important events and attitudes of the 1950s.

A typical episode included:
» a musical act, usually a significant artist that opened the show with multiple musical numbers;
» performances by comedians of the time;
» scenes or songs from major Broadway musicals;
» interviews with major sports, cultural, or political figures;
» performances such as puppet shows, animal acts, and circus acts;
» dances or other performances from ballerinas or other notable performers; and
» a concluding musical act.

Your task: Based on your understanding of the 1950s, compile a schedule for one episode of *The Ed Sullivan Show* that depicts major influential cultural figures who shaped American identity or values in the 1950s.
» Research and choose the 8–10 acts that will appear on the show.
» Write a justification for including these acts that explains their significance in American culture and their importance to American identity in the 1950s.
» Write a set of questions for Ed Sullivan to ask each performer or group after its performance. What would the American public want to know about this group or person? What are the concerns or interests of 1950s Americans about this group or person?
» Write an opening monologue for Ed Sullivan about the show for the night, what people will see, and why they should be excited to stay tuned.
» You may include any figures from the decade and you are not restricted to the ones you listened to or read about in the unit. You may expand your research to include authors, music groups, sports figures, political figures, actors, or any other significant individuals you find from the 1950s. You may not copy the schedule of an actual episode of the show.

Present your show in PowerPoint or another format. Include photos of each act, your interview questions, and music and/or clips as appropriate.

LESSON 2

Robots and Martians

Alignment of Unit Goals

» Goal 1: To understand the concept of identity in 1950s America.

» Goal 2: To develop skills in historical analysis and song and artwork interpretation.

» Goal 3: To develop analytical and interpretive skills in literature.

» Goal 4: To develop an understanding of historical events occurring in the United States during the 1950s.

Unit Objectives

» To describe how changes in American identity in the 1950s are revealed in the music, art, and literature of the decade;

» To define the context in which a song or piece of art was produced and the implications of context for understanding the artifact;

» To describe a writer's or artist's intent in producing a given song or piece of art based on understanding of text and context;

» To describe what a selected literary passage means;

» To cite similarities and differences in meaning among selected works of literature; and

» To describe music, art, and literature of the 1950s that reflected the American identity.

Resources for Unit Implementation

» **Handout 2.1:** Literature Analysis Model

» **Handout 2.2:** Science Fiction Story Analysis

» **Handout 2.3:** Aliens!

» **Handout 2.4:** Technology Changes America

» **Read:** "Franchise" by Isaac Asimov (1953a)

» **Read:** "Nobody Here But…" by Isaac Asimov (1953b). An online version is available at http://www.e-book2u.net/book/205/Isaac Asimov.

» **Read:** "There Will Come Soft Rains" by Ray Bradbury (1950)

» **View:** Art of Arthur Radebaugh. The art is available online at http://www.smithsonian.com/radebaugh.

» **Read:** "Youth" by Isaac Asimov (1955)

» **Read:** "The Concrete Mixer" by Ray Bradbury (1951a)

» **Read:** "Zero Hour" by Ray Bradbury (1951b)

» **Watch:** Disneyland "House of the Future" video. Available on YouTube at http://www.youtube.com/watch?v=DoCCO3GKqWY.

Key Terms

» *Science fiction*: a genre of fiction dealing with future settings and imagined content
» *Technology*: any new tool developed to solve a problem

Learning Experiences

1. Explain to students that during WWII, the first computers were created to break coded messages being used by the opposing military forces. After the war, many people speculated on the possibilities that this new technology presented. The genre of science fiction expanded and became more popular.

2. Divide students into groups of three in preparation for a modified jigsaw activity. In their groups, have each student select one of the following stories to read: "Franchise" or "Nobody Here But…" by Isaac Asimov (1953a, 1953b), or "There Will Come Soft Rains" by Ray Bradbury (1950). Each student will read a different story and report back to the group. Have each student analyze his or her story using the Literature Analysis Model (Handout 2.1) and the following questions. **Ask:** What new use of computers is the story about? At the outset, how did people view the new technology? What happens in the story to alter that view? What fears does the story reveal about technology in American society? Students should record all information about the three stories on the Science Fiction Story Analysis sheet (Handout 2.2).

3. After students have read and shared their story and responses, have them **discuss** as a group: What threats to American values or American identity do the stories express?

4. Watch "House of the Future" from Disneyland on YouTube. **Ask:** What does this video say are the drawbacks with 1950s houses? What is the house of the future like? What will technology do to improve homes in the future?

5. Have students view the art of Arthur Radebaugh. **Ask:** What attitude toward new technology does this reveal? How does this image fit with the Bradbury story "There Will Come Soft Rains"? What do these two different points of view reveal about American attitudes toward technology?

6. Have students read either "Youth" by Isaac Asimov (1955) or "The Concrete Mixer" or "Zero Hour" by Ray Bradbury (1951a, 1951b). Give students the Aliens! sheet (Handout 2.3) and **discuss:** How are creatures from other planets viewed in the story? What is the

relationship between the aliens and humans? How do the humans view and treat the aliens in the story? Why is this? What American values or identity traits does this story reveal? How do these images of aliens match with modern versions of aliens seen in TV and movies? How are the images similar and how are they different? Why is this?

7. To summarize the ideas from the stories, have students use the Identity Chart from Lesson 1 (Handout 1.1) for the U.S. in 1944. Students should then complete the Technology Changes America sheet (Handout 2.4). Discuss student responses in small groups and then aloud with the large group. **Ask:** How is American identity changing with new technology? How does the new technology affect or alter the culture and values seen in the stories? How do new technology and its possibilities affect our international role? In what ways are the possibilities of the new technology simply extensions of our historic traditions and patterns?

8. Pose the following questions for a large-group discussion. **Ask:** Which of the technologies described in the stories have been achieved? Have those achieved technologies had the outcomes predicted in the stories? Do we have similar views and concerns about technology and potential new technologies today? Why or why not? How have American attitudes toward technology and American identity changed since the 1950s when these stories were written? Why?

9. Continue the large-group discussion. **Ask:** In what year were many of the stories set? Have students write a short story about the future and where they think technology will be 50 years from the present day and how it will affect the identity of the American public.

Assessing Student Learning

» Literature Analysis Model
» Science Fiction Story Analysis
» Aliens! activity
» Technology Changes America activity
» Discussions

Extending Student Learning

The following are optional activities for extending student learning in this lesson:
» Have the student design a house of the future for the year 2050. Have the student include information about the rationale for each design feature.
» Have the student review the reading selections from this lesson and compare the ideas included to the present state of the U.S. in terms of technology advances.

Name:_____ Date: _____

HANDOUT 2.1
Literature Analysis Model

Directions: Complete the boxes below to analyze the short story you read.

Chosen or assigned text: _____	
Key words:	
Important ideas:	
Tone:	
Mood:	
Imagery:	
Symbolism:	
Structure of writing:	

Name:_____ Date:_____

HANDOUT 2.2
Science Fiction Story Analysis

Directions: Answer the following questions for all three science fiction stories.

Asimov: "Nobody Here But . . ."	Asimov: "Franchise"	Bradbury: "There Will Come Soft Rains"
What new use of computers is the story about?		
At the outset, how do people view the new technology?		
What happens in the story to alter that view?		
What fears does the story reveal about technology in American society?		

Name:_____ Date:_____

HANDOUT 2.3
Aliens!

Directions: Answer the following questions.

1. Which story did you read?

2. How are creatures from other planets viewed in the story?

3. What is the relationship between the aliens and humans? How do the humans view and treat the aliens in the story? Why is this?

4. What American values or identity traits does this story reveal?

Handout 2.3: Aliens!, continued

5. What does this story reveal about how Americans in the 1950s viewed changing technology bilities? How did they view themselves?

6. How do these images of aliens match with modern versions of aliens seen in TV and movies? How are these images similar and how are they different?

7. What do modern images of aliens tell us about how we view ourselves and the world?

8. What has changed for the U.S. since the 1950s to explain these changing views on aliens? What does it say about us as Americans that we continue to tell stories of people from other planets?

Name: _____ Date: _____

HANDOUT 2.4

Technology Changes America

Directions: Complete the circles below by answering the questions in them.

How does the new technology affect or have the possibility of altering our culture and values?

How does new technology and its possibilities affect our international role?

The Role of Technology in Identity in the Nuclear Age

In what ways are the possibilities of the new technology simply extensions of our historic traditions and patterns?

How does the new technology affect the economy?

LESSON 3

The Red Scare and McCarthyism

Alignment of Unit Goals

» Goal 1: To understand the concept of identity in 1950s America.
» Goal 2: To develop skills in historical analysis and song and artwork interpretation.
» Goal 3: To develop analytical and interpretive skills in literature.
» Goal 4: To develop an understanding of historical events occurring in the United States during the 1950s.

Unit Objectives

» To describe how changes in American identity in the 1950s are revealed in the music, art, and literature of the decade;
» To describe a writer's or artist's intent in producing a given song or piece of art based on understanding of text and context.
» To consider short- and long-term consequences of a given document/artifact;
» To describe what a selected literary passage means;
» To cite similarities and differences in meaning among selected works of literature;
» To make inferences based on information in given passages;
» To describe major historical events during the 1950s that affected the American identity; and
» To describe music, art, and literature of the 1950s that reflected the American identity.

Resources for Unit Implementation

»   **Handout 3.1:** Primary Source Document Analysis Model

»   **Handout 3.2:** Literature Analysis Model

»   **Handout 3.3:** Music Analysis Model

»   **Handout 3.4:** Identity During the Red Scare

»   **Read:** Joseph McCarthy's (1950) speech from Wheeling, WV. The speech is available online at http://historymatters.gmu.edu/d/6456/.

»   **Read:** "Ballad of the Noble Intentions," "Little Ballad for Americans," and "Political Prisoner 123456789," by Edwin Rolfe (1953a, 1953b, 1953c). "Ballad of the Noble Intentions" can be found on Google Books at http://www.books.google.com/books?id=GodSI0E2 y8MC&pg=PA123&source=gbs_toc_r&cad=4#v=onepage&q&f=false. "Political Prisoner 123456789" can also be found via Google Books at http://www.books.google.com.boo ks?id=GodSI0E2y8MC&pg=PA126&source=gbs_toc_r&cad=4#v=onepage&q&f=false. "Little Ballad for Americans" can be found at http://www.unionsong.com/u659.html.

»   **Read:** A choice of:
    ○   *The Adventures of Robin Hood* by Roger Lancelyn Green (2010);
    ○   *Fahrenheit 451* by Ray Bradbury (1953):
    ○   *Civil Disobedience* by Henry David Thoreau (1849); or
    ○   *1984* by George Orwell (1949).

»   **Listen:** "Wasn't That a Time" by Pete Seeger (1955). The song is available on YouTube at http://www.youtube.com/watch?v=3rYyTAX-I3w.

»   **Listen:** "Get That Communist, Joe" (Weinman & Dorney, 1954) by The Kavaliers. The song is available on YouTube at http://www.youtube.com/watch?v=MzKW-oz1Lbw.

»   **Read:** "Don't Join the Book Burners!" from the comments of President Dwight D. Eisenhower (1953) at the Dartmouth College Commencement. The full speech is available at http://www.presidency.ucsb.edu/ws/?pid=9606.

Key Terms

»   *McCarthyism:* making accusations of disloyalty or subversion without evidence; the term was named after U.S. Senator Joseph McCarthy of Wisconsin because of his anti-Communist concerns
»   *Red Scare:* the concern about the rise of Communism

Learning Experiences

1. Explain to students that along with a fear of the atomic bomb and creatures from other planets, there was also a fear of a communist takeover of the United States. The rhetoric of the communist revolution in Russia and the rest of the Soviet Union called for a worldwide revolution and the spread of communist ideals, but communism conflicted

with American values such as democracy, individualism, personal success, and religion. Review information about Senator Joseph McCarthy, the House Un-American Activities Committee (HUAC), and the Red Scare from any of the recommended history texts. Have students read McCarthy's 1950 speech in Wheeling, WV, and analyze it using the Primary Source Document Analysis Model sheet (Handout 3.1).

2. Explain to students that during the Red Scare, Senator McCarthy and HUAC investigated government officials, Hollywood directors, screenwriters, actors, and authors whom they suspected either had communist ties or were helping the communist effort. Certain books were banned and removed from libraries.

3. Have students read either a story or book from the choices of: *The Adventures of Robin Hood* (Green, 2010), *Fahrenheit 451* (Bradbury, 1953), *Civil Disobedience* (Thoreau, 1849), or *1984* (Orwell, 1949). Analyze it with the Literature Analysis Model (Handout 3.2). **Ask:** What is the plot or message of the book or story? Explain that each of these was removed from libraries or blacklisted for being anti-American during the Red Scare. Why might this book be blacklisted? What in this book or story might be considered anti-American or pro-communist? Do these books represent a threat to American identity or American values? In what way does the book or story support American values? Why, given the other events of the time, might these books be seen as dangerous or subversive? What does the willingness of the American public to ban and remove these books from libraries reveal about America in the 1950s? Do Senator McCarthy's views and the practice of blacklisting books contradict American values? Why or why not? **Ask:** Do you think most people supported Senator McCarthy and his work to expose and get rid of communist elements in the U.S.? Why or why not?

4. Have students read the poems of Edwin Rolfe (1953a, 1953b, 1953c). Have them complete a Literature Analysis Model (Handout 3.2) and discuss their responses as a large group. **Ask:** How does Edwin Rolfe seem to feel about Senator McCarthy's actions? What do the poems suggest about why people supported Senator McCarthy? Are McCarthy's actions changing attitudes? Accusing innocent men? Dividing the identity of the U.S.?

5. Explain to students that one of the people called before HUAC was the folk singer Pete Seeger. In his interview, he was repeatedly asked about a song he sang on July 4, 1955. Have students read and listen to Pete Seeger's (1955) "Wasn't That a Time" and analyze the song using the Music Analysis Model (Handout 3.3). The Kavaliers also had a song about Senator McCarthy. Have students listen and analyze the song "Get that Communist, Joe" (Weinman & Dorney, 1954) by The Kavaliers. **Ask:** How are these two songs similar? How are these songs different? How do they depict Senator McCarthy's actions? What do they feel are the effects of Senator McCarthy's investigations on the U.S.? What do these songs reveal about how Americans felt about the Red Scare? Although many Americans feared the Soviet Union, do you think they all agreed with Senator McCarthy? Why or why not?

6. Explain that in 1953, President Dwight D. Eisenhower made a speech at the commencement at Dartmouth College that said the following:

> Don't join the book burners! Don't think you're going to conceal faults by concealing evidence that they ever existed. Don't be afraid to go in your library and read every book, as long as any document does not offend our own ideas of decency. That should be the only censorship.

How will we defeat communism unless we know what it is, what it teaches? And why does it have such an appeal for men, why are so many people swearing allegiance to it? It's almost a religion, albeit one of the nether regions.

And we have got to fight it with something better, not try to conceal the thinking of our own people. They are part of America. And even if they think ideas that are contrary to ours, their right to say them, their right to record them, and their right to have them at places where they're accessible to others is unquestioned or it's not America. (Eisenhower, 1953)

Ask: What is the message of the President? What does it tell us about the Red Scare and McCarthyism from President Eisenhower's perspective? How much does President Eisenhower reflect the view of most Americans in the 1950s? What American values is the President stressing in his remarks?

7. Have students analyze the effects of McCarthyism on the United States using the Identity During the Red Scare sheet (Handout 3.4). Discuss student responses in the large group. Review with students the downfall of Senator McCarthy and explain that although the investigation ended, many of those blacklisted remained so until 1960 or later. **Ask:** How do the actions of Senator McCarthy and HUAC and the American response to the Red Scare fit with American values and identity? How do they contradict American values and identity? What does the end of the Red Scare and the HUAC hearings reveal about America?

Assessing Student Learning

- » Primary Source Document Analysis Model
- » Literature Analysis Model
- » Music Analysis Model
- » Identity During the Red Scare activity
- » Discussions

Extending Student Learning

The following are optional activities for extending student learning in this lesson:

- » Have students identify personal foci of protest regarding some feature of American politics or society. The students may write their own protest songs or poetry, or develop artwork. Possible topics might include: poverty, gang violence, drug abuse, sexism, racism, etc.
- » The arts may also be used to express patriotism. Have students write their own songs or poetry, or develop artwork expressing patriotic feelings for the United States.

HANDOUT 3.1

Primary Source Document
Analysis Model

Directions: Analyze Senator Joseph McCarthy's speech by completing the boxes below.

Document: _____

What is the title of the document? Why was it given this title?

Title:
Why do you think it was given this title?
Which words in the title are especially important? Why?

What is your reaction to the document?

What is the first thing about this document that draws your attention?
What is in the document that surprises you, or that you didn't expect?

Handout 3.1: Primary Source Document Analysis Model, continued

What are some of the powerful ideas expressed in the document?
What feelings does the primary source cause in you?
What questions does it raise for you?

When was the document written? Why was it written?

Who is the author(s)?
When was the document written?
What do you know about the culture of the time period in which the document was written?

What were the important events occurring at the time the document was written?
What was the author's purpose in writing this document?
Who is the intended audience?
What biases do you see in the author's text?

What are the important ideas in this document?

What problems or events does the document address?
What is the author's main point or argument?

What actions or outcomes does the author expect? From whom?
How do you think this author would define *American identity*? What elements of the American identity does the author see as being threatened or cultivated? Why?

What is your evaluation of this document?

Is this document authentic? How do you know?
Is this author a reliable source for addressing this issue/problem?
How representative is this document of the views of the people at this time in history?
How does this document compare with others of the same time period?

Name:_____ Date: _____

What could have been the possible consequences of this document?
What actually happened as a result of this document? Discuss the long-term, short-term, and unintended consequences.
What interpretation of this historical period does this document provide?
How does this document contribute to your understanding of the American identity during this time period?

Name:_____ Date: _____

HANDOUT 3.2
Literature Analysis Model

Directions: Analyze the story you read by completing the boxes below.

Chosen or assigned text: _____	
Key words:	
Important ideas:	
Tone:	
Mood:	
Imagery:	
Symbolism:	
Structure of writing:	

HANDOUT 3.3

Music Analysis Model

Directions: Complete the boxes below after listening to the assigned songs.

Song Title:_____

What is the title of the song? Why was it given this title?

Title:
Why do you think it was given this title?
Which words in the title are especially important? Why?

What is your reaction to the song?

What is the first thing about this song that draws your attention?
What is in the song that surprises you, or that you didn't expect?
What are some of the powerful ideas expressed in the song?
What feelings does the song cause in you?
What questions does it raise for you?

Name:_____ Date: _____

When was the song written? Why was it written?

Who is the songwriter(s)?
When was the song written?
What is the song's purpose? To entertain? To dance to? To critique something?
What were the important events occurring at the time the song was written?
Who is the intended audience?
What biases do you see in the author's lyrics?

What are the important ideas in this song?

Lyrics	Music/Accompaniment
What is the subject of the song? Summarize the song.	Describe the music or melody of this song. Is it fast-paced or slow? Does it have low notes or high notes? Is it melodic or does it have lots of percussion?
What are the main points of the song? What is the song saying about the subject?	What feelings do you get from the music? Why?
What mood/values/feelings does the singer have about the topic?	How does the tone or mood of the music fit with the lyrics? Why might this be?

What is your evaluation of this song?

What new or different interpretation of this historical period does this song provide?
What does this song portray about American identity or how Americans felt at the time?

HANDOUT 3.4
Identity During the Red Scare

Directions: Analyze the effects of McCarthyism by answering the questions below.

Identity changes with new ideas, experiences, conditions, or in response to other expressions of identity.
What new conditions or identities were Americans being confronted with during the Red Scare?
How did the ideas of communism cause Americans to reexamine or change their own identity? Why?
How did confronting the ideas of communism change American identity? In what ways did American identity remain the same in the face of communist ideas?
There are multiple elements of identity and at different times, different elements have greater or lesser importance.
During the Red Scare, what elements of identity were being stressed? What American values or traits were Senator McCarthy and others focused on?
What elements of American identity seem to have been ignored or reduced in importance? What American values or traits were being contradicted or sacrificed during the Red Scare? Why is this?
What lessons can we learn from this historical period about promoting and preserving identities and values?

Name:_____ Date: _____

Although members of a group or society may have different individual identities, they still share particular elements of identity.

What shared elements of identity were found in the Red Scare? What different elements of identity appeared in the events of the Red Scare?

What does it tell us about America in the 1950s that, despite the divided nation, the fear of communism, and Senator McCarthy's remarks, Americans still shared similar traits and values?

LESSON 4

Soda Fountains and Levittowns

Alignment of Unit Goals

» Goal 1: To understand the concept of identity in 1950s America.

» Goal 2: To develop skills in historical analysis and song and artwork interpretation.

» Goal 4: To develop an understanding of historical events occurring in the United States during the 1950s.

Unit Objectives

» To describe how changes in American identity in the 1950s are revealed in the music, art, and literature of the decade;

» To define the context in which a song or piece of art was produced and the implications of context for understanding the artifact;

» To analyze the effects of given documents or artifacts on the interpretation of historical events;

» To describe major historical events during the 1950s that affected the American identity; and

» To describe music, art, and literature of the 1950s that reflected the American identity.

Resources for Unit Implementation

» **Handout 4.1:** Levittowns

» **Handout 4.2:** Music Analysis Model

» **Handout 4.3:** 1950s Identity Chart

» **Handout 4.4:** *The Man in the Gray Flannel Suit*

> » **Read:** *Levittown: Documents of an Ideal American Suburb* (Hales, 2013). Documents are available at http://tigger.uic.edu/~pbhales/Levittown.

> » **Listen:** "I Can Dream, Can't I" (Fain, 1938) by The Andrew Sisters; "Goodnight Irene" (Ledbetter, 1934) by The Weavers; "How High the Moon" (Hamilton & Lewis, 1940) by Les Paul; "Come On-a My House" (Bagdasarian & Saroyan, 1951) by Rosemary Clooney; "Wheel of Fortune" (Benjamin & Weiss, 1951) by Kay Starr; "Because of You" (Hammerstein & Wilkinson, 1940) by Tony Bennett. All songs are available on YouTube.

> » **Watch:** YouTube clips from television shows *The Adventures of Ozzie & Harriet* and/or *Leave It to Beaver*. No one specific clip has to be shown, and there are many to choose from on YouTube.

> » **Read:** Excerpts from *The Man in the Gray Flannel Suit* by Sloan Wilson (1955). Excerpts are available at http://www.umsl.edu/virtualstl/phase2/1950/events/perspectives/documents/flannelexp.html. (*Note:* If the full text is available, have students read the entire text instead of just the excerpts provided in the link.)

Key Terms

> » *Suburb*: a residential area outside a city
> » *Levittown*: suburban development in which identical homes were produced for returning veterans and first-time homebuyers
> » *Conformity*: matching one's behaviors and attitudes to a group's norms
> » *Soda fountain*: a machine that dispenses carbonated soft drinks. Soda fountains located in pharmacies and ice cream parlors became public places where people could socialize.

Learning Experiences

1. **Ask:** What things come to mind when you hear the words "1950s in America"? What images, trends, or artifacts do you think of? For many people today, they think of poodle skirts, jukeboxes, and *Happy Days* and *Grease*. Explain that in this lesson, students will look at the source of these popular images and what they reveal about American identity and the American experience in the 1950s.

2. Explain to students that after World War II, there was a growth of the suburban areas of America. This was due largely to more affordable mortgages established by the G.I. Bill and to a buildup of wealth and technology during the war. People were moving out of the cities in large numbers to single family homes with yards. In this lesson, students will look at some of these new housing developments.

3. Have students go to the "Levittown: Documents of an Ideal American Suburb" website. Follow the links to "Building Levittown: A Primer," "Unfinished: Expanding and Decorating Levittown," "Original Photographs of '50s Levittown From the Family Collection of Charles F. Tekula, Jr.," and "Original Photographs of '50s and '60s Levittown from the Family Collection of Carl A. 'Rusty' Arnesen." Have students complete Levittowns (Handout 4.1). **Ask:** What is Levittown? What is life in these communities like? What are the homes like? What identity is being created in the developments like Levittown? How much of this identity is reality? Why is this a desired identity? Who desires it? What values or beliefs about America do we see in Levittowns?

4. Give students a Music Analysis Model (Handout 4.2) and play for students the songs "I Can Dream, Can't I" (Fain, 1938) by The Andrew Sisters; "Goodnight Irene" (Ledbetter, 1934) by

The Weavers; "How High the Moon" (Hamilton & Lewis, 1940) by Les Paul; "Come On-a My House" (Bagdasarian & Saroyan, 1951) by Rosemary Clooney; "Wheel of Fortune" (Benjamin & Weiss, 1951) by Kay Starr; or "Because of You" (Hammerstein & Wilkinson, 1940) by Tony Bennett. Explain that all of these songs were top sellers and radio-play songs in 1950–1952. **Ask:** What identity is being promoted by these songs—what lifestyle, priorities, values, concerns? What do these songs suggest about the mood or common culture of America in the 1950s? How does the mood of these songs compare to the songs about atomic bombs we heard in Lesson 1? How is it that both groups of songs could be popular and listened to at the same time?

5. Explain to students that popular TV shows of the time included *The Adventures of Ozzie & Harriet* and *Leave It to Beaver*. These shows focused on suburban families in which the dad worked, the mom stayed home and cooked and cleaned, and the kids were cute, occasionally in trouble, but overall well behaved. Episodes of both shows are available on YouTube and segments could be shown if desired. Based on the songs and the Levittown website, have students complete the 1950s Identity Chart (Handout 4.3). Review student responses in small groups, then as a large group.

6. Have students read *The Man in the Gray Flannel Suit* by Sloan Wilson (1955) and give students the *The Man in the Gray Flannel Suit* sheet (Handout 4.4). **Ask:** What is happening in the story? In what ways are Tom and Betsy typical Americans of the postwar years? How do they display the identity of Levittowns and suburban America at the beginning? How do Tom and Betsy really feel about their lives? Why? Where do you see evidence of this? How do Tom and Betsy change over the course of the story? What do they end up doing? What does this book suggest about the American identity created in TV and Levittowns? To what extent does conformity to these ideals really exist?

7. **Ask:** The 1950s is often called "The Age of Conformity." Do you think this is an accurate description? Why or why not? To what extent is the conformity real and to what extent is it an aspiration or construction? What does the concept of conformity tell us about American culture and identity?

Assessing Student Learning

- » Levittowns activity
- » Music Analysis Model
- » 1950s Identity Chart
- » *The Man in the Gray Flannel Suit* activity

Extending Student Learning

The following are optional activities for extending student learning in this lesson:

- » Have students research information about the consumer culture in America based on the automobile industry in the 1950s. Have the students prepare a presentation or other resource to share the information with their classmates.
- » Have students research the Federal-Aid Highway Act of 1956. (President Eisenhower signed the bill into law in 1956, building a nationwide highway network of 41,000 miles of roads.) More information can be found at http://nationalatlas.gov/articles/transportation/a_highway.html. Have students prepare an analysis of how this legislation encouraged the growth of suburbs and the rise of the automobile industry.

Name:_____ Date:_____

HANDOUT 4.1
Levittowns

Directions: Go to "Levittown: Documents of an Ideal American Suburb" at http://tigger.uic.edu/~pbhales/
Levittown. Click on "Building Levittown: A Primer;" "Unfinished: Expanding and Decorating Levittown;" "Original
Photographs of '50s Levittown from the Family Collection of Charles F. Tekula, Jr.;" and "Original Photographs of '50s
and '60s Levittown from the Family Collection of Carl A. 'Rusty' Arnesen." Answer the questions below.

1. What was Levittown?

2. What was life in these communities like?

3. What were the homes like?

4. What identity was being created in the developments like Levittown?

5. How much of this identity was reality? Why was this a desired identity? Who desired it?

6. What values or beliefs about America and what it means to be an American do we see in Levittowns?

Name: _____ Date: _____

Music Analysis Model

Directions: Complete the boxes below after listening to the assigned songs.

Song Title: _____

What is the title of the song? Why was it given this title?

Title:
Why do you think it was given this title?
Which words in the title are especially important? Why?

What is your reaction to the song?

What is the first thing about this song that draws your attention?
What is in the song that surprises you, or that you didn't expect?
What are some of the powerful ideas expressed in the song?
What feelings does the song cause in you?
What questions does it raise for you?

Name:_____ Date: _____

When was the song written? Why was it written?

Who is the songwriter(s)?
When was the song written?
What is the song's purpose? To entertain? To dance to? To critique something?
What were the important events occurring at the time the song was written?
Who is the intended audience?
What biases do you see in the author's lyrics?

What are the important ideas in this song?

Lyrics	Music/Accompaniment
What is the subject of the song? Summarize the song.	Describe the music or melody of this song. Is it fast-paced or slow? Does it have low notes or high notes? Is it melodic or does it have lots of percussion?
What are the main points of the song? What is the song saying about the subject?	What feelings do you get from the music? Why?
What mood/values/feelings does the singer have about the topic?	How does the tone or mood of the music fit with the lyrics? Why might this be?

What is your evaluation of this song?

What new or different interpretation of this historical period does this song provide?
What does this song portray about American identity or how Americans felt at the time?

HANDOUT 4.3
1950s Identity Chart

Directions: Using the songs you listened to and the Levittown website, complete the chart by answering the questions below.

Identity changes with new ideas, experiences, conditions, or in response to other expressions of identity.
What new ideas, experiences, or conditions were Americans facing in the 1950s? How was this changing American identity? What new characteristics were being introduced? What traits of identity were being altered or lost?

Identity is created, either by a group or person or by outsiders, and self-created identities may be different from how others see one's self.
What identity was being created in American society in the 1950s? What identity were those who move to Levittowns creating? Who might have been an outsider to this identity? How might these outsiders have viewed those who lived in Levittowns and identified with this music? Why?

There are multiple elements of identity and at different times, different elements have greater or lesser importance.
During the war, nationalism took precedence. What elements of identity were or seemed to be more important to people in the 1950s? Why was this?

Although members of a group or society may have different individual identities, they still share particular elements of identity.
Did all segments of American society live in Levittowns and listen to this type of music? Why or why not? What did the popularity of these songs and houses (like those in Levittowns) reveal about the traits all Americans shared in the 1950s?

HANDOUT 4.4

The Man in the Gray Flannel Suit

Directions: Answer the questions below.

1. What is happening in the story? What are Tom and Betsy doing in the beginning of the story? How do they display the identity of Levittowns and suburban America at the beginning of the story? How do Tom and Betsy really feel about their lives? Why?

2. In what ways are Tom and Betsy typical Americans of the postwar years? How are they different from the ideals and identity being portrayed in the 1950s?

3. What does this book suggest about the American identity created in TV and Levittowns? To what extent does conformity to these ideals really exist? What does that tell us about American identity and values in the 1950s? Do most Americans desire a particular set of traits despite reality?

Civil Rights in the 1950s

Alignment of Unit Goals

» Goal 1: To understand the concept of identity in 1950s America.

» Goal 2: To develop skills in historical analysis and song and artwork interpretation.

» Goal 3: To develop analytical and interpretive skills in literature.

» Goal 4: To develop an understanding of historical events occurring in the United States during the 1950s.

Unit Objectives:

» To describe how the American identity changed during the 1950s;

» To describe how changes in American identity in the 1950s are revealed in the music, art, and literature of the decade;

» To define the context in which a song or piece of art was produced and the implications of context for understanding the artifact;

» To describe a writer's or artist's intent in producing a given song or piece of art based on understanding of text and context;

» To consider short- and long-term consequences of a given document or artifact;

» To describe what a selected literary passage means; and

» To describe major historical events during the 1950s that affected the American identity.

Resources for Unit Implementation:

» **Handout 5.1:** Music Analysis Model

» **Handout 5.2:** Questions: *Invisible Man*

» **Handout 5.3:** Identity of Civil Rights

» **Research:** *Brown v. Board of Education*. Information is available at http://www.pbs.org/wnet/supremecourt/rights/landmark_brown.html.

» **Research:** Rosa Parks and the Montgomery Bus boycott. Information is available at http://mlk-kpp01.stanford.edu/index.php/encyclopedia/encyclopedia/enc_montgomery_bus_boycott_1955_1956/.

» **Research:** The formation of the Southern Christian Leadership Conference. Information is available at http://mlk-kpp01.stanford.edu/index.php/encyclopedia/encyclopedia/enc_southern_christian_leadership_conference_sclc/.

» **Research:** W. E. B. DuBois, Booker T. Washington, and A. Philip Randolph. Information about all three figures can be found at http://www.pbs.org/wnet/jimcrow/stories_people.html.

» **Read:** "Harlem" by Langston Hughes (1951/1990). The poem is available online at http://www.poetryfoundation.org/poem/175884.

» **Listen:** "We Are Americans Too" by Nat King Cole (2009). The song can be listened to at http://www.rhapsody.com/artist/nat-king-cole/album/voices-of-change-then-and-now/track/we-are-americans-too-featuring-excerpt-from-president-barack.

» **Read:** The prologue, Chapter 12, Chapter 13, Chapter 16, and Chapter 23 from *Invisible Man* by Ralph Ellison (1952). Excerpts are available at http://www. bpi.edu/ourpages/auto/2010/5/11/36901472/Ralph%20Ellison%20-%20Invisible%20Man%20v3_0.pdf.

Key Terms

» *Civil rights*: rights that protect one's individual freedoms within a society

Learning Experiences

1. Explain to students that suburban life was not the experience of all Americans. African Americans faced economic, social, and political discrimination. During the 1950s, a series of events took place that increased the demand for increased civil rights for African Americans. Using a history text or the resources provided in "Resources for Unit Implementation", review *Brown v. Board of Education*, Rosa Parks and the Montgomery Bus boycott, and the formation of the Southern Christian Leadership Conference. Explain that pressure for increased rights for African Americans had been building since the Reconstruction in the late 19th century, when W. E. B. DuBois and Booker T. Washington had both advocated for increased rights.

2. **Ask:** If African Americans had been seeking greater equality for decades, why was there a greater demand and the chance for success in the 1950s? What new experiences had America gone through in the last several decades that explain the changes in American identity and increased involvement of African Americans?

3. Have students read the Langston Hughes (1951/1990) poem "Harlem." **Ask:** What is the dream to which Langston Hughes is referring? What is the message of the poem? How

does this explain why the Civil Rights Movement gained momentum in the mid-1950s?

4. The question most African Americans had was how to organize the Civil Rights Movement. There had been different philosophies of how to achieve equality for many years. Booker T. Washington and W. E. B. DuBois had opposing views at the turn of the century, and the 1950s were no different. Have students listen to "We are Americans Too" by Nat King Cole (2009). This song was released posthumously and not in 1956, when it was written and recorded, because Capitol Records refused to release it then. Have students analyze the songs using the Music Analysis Model (Handout 5.1). **Ask:** What does this song suggest about how to approach the fight for increased rights? What approach does it promote and why? Why do you think Capitol Records refused to release the song in 1956?

5. Have students read the excerpts from *Invisible Man* by Ralph Ellison (1952) and answer the questions on Handout 5.2. (*Note:* This novel contains mature language that may be offensive. The teacher should read the material ahead of time and decide whether it is appropriate for his or her students.) **Ask:** How does Ellison's view of civil rights and the method of achieving these rights compare to the views of Martin Luther King, Jr. or Nat King Cole? How are they similar and how are they different? Why might this be?

6. Have students complete the Identity of Civil Rights chart (Handout 5.3) and discuss student responses as a large group.

Assessing Student Learning

- » Music Analysis Model
- » *Invisible Man* questions
- » Identity of Civil Rights activity
- » Discussion

Extending Student Learning

The following are optional activities for extending student learning in this lesson:

- » Have students read *Warriors Don't Cry: A Searing Memoir of the Battle to Integrate Little Rock's Central High* by Melba Pattillo Beals (2001). Have them prepare an overview of the book, connecting it to what has been studied in this lesson.
- » Have students research 1957's Executive Order 10730: Desegregation of Central High School. Information can be found at http://ourdocuments.gov/doc.php?flash=true&doc=89. Have them prepare a summary of the order, including its impact on life in 1950s America.
- » Have students locate information about the "Little Rock Nine." Have them prepare a song, poem, or piece of art depicting the role of those students in the Civil Rights Movement.

Name:_____ Date:_____

HANDOUT 5.1
Music Analysis Model

Directions: Complete the boxes below after listening to the assigned songs.

Song Title:_____

What is the title of the song? Why was it given this title?

Title:
Why do you think it was given this title?
Which words in the title are especially important? Why?

What is your reaction to the song?

What is the first thing about this song that draws your attention?
What is in the song that surprises you, or that you didn't expect?
What are some of the powerful ideas expressed in the song?
What feelings does the song cause in you?
What questions does it raise for you?

Name:_____ Date: _____

When was the song written? Why was it written?

Who is the songwriter(s)?
When was the song written?
What is the song's purpose? To entertain? To dance to? To critique something?
What were the important events occurring at the time the song was written?
Who is the intended audience?
What biases do you see in the author's lyrics?

What are the important ideas in this song?

Lyrics	Music/Accompaniment
What is the subject of the song? Summarize the song.	Describe the music or melody of this song. Is it fast-paced or slow? Does it have low notes or high notes? Is it melodic or does it have lots of percussion?
What are the main points of the song? What is the song saying about the subject?	What feelings do you get from the music? Why?
What mood/values/feelings does the singer have about the topic?	How does the tone or mood of the music fit with the lyrics? Why might this be?

What is your evaluation of this song?

What new or different interpretation of this historical period does this song provide?
What does this song portray about American identity or how Americans felt at the time?

HANDOUT 5.2
Invisible Man

Directions: Answer the questions below.

Prologue

1. What does the protagonist mean when he says he is invisible?

2. What does the last paragraph mean?

3. How does this excerpt describe relations between the races?

Chapter 12

1. How does the woman in the chapter view relations between the races?

2. Why does she feel Southern African Americans need to make the change?

3. What does the chapter reveal about African American attitudes and identity in the 1950s?

Chapter 13

1. What is happening in this chapter?

2. When the narrator starts talking to the crowd he keeps saying, "We're law-abiding" and refers to a man in Alabama. Why? What is his point in reiterating these ideas? What seems to be his point of view on the movement in Alabama? Is he really encouraging the crowd to be law-abiding?

3. The narrator also keeps talking about being "dispossessed." What does he mean that the crowd is all dispossessed? What is the author's point?

4. He talks about the old folks' "dream book." What were the names he calls it? What values or identity do these names stress?

5. What does this chapter reveal about the identity or views of African Americans in the 1950s?

Chapter 16

1. What does the narrator mean when he says African Americans are "uncommon people"?

2. What does he feel African Americans let the rest of America do to them?

3. What is the point of the blind man story?

4. What is he calling on the crowd to do?

5. What does he mean when he says he is becoming more human?

Handout 5.2: *The Invisible Man,* continued

6. Brother Jack (a White leader of the organization the narrator works for) says "don't end your usefulness before you've begun." What does this mean? What does this say about how Whites who seemed to support the Civil Rights Movement really felt about African Americans?

7. What changes in African American identity is the author calling for? Is he asking them to change their self-created identity or the identity created for them by others? Why do you think this?

Chapter 23

1. How does the narrator view Whites working for the organization to promote African American rights? How has his view of these Whites changed through the book? Why?

2. As a result, how has the narrator come to view the movement for civil rights? Why doesn't he feel he can organize his own group or movement?

3. What does this reveal about the identity of African Americans in the 1950s? How uniform is that identity across all African Americans? Why?

4. How does the African American experience in this book compare to the experiences of Whites in America that we have been studying in previous lessons? What traits or experiences do the races have in common? What is different? Why is this?

HANDOUT 5.3
Identity of Civil Rights

Directions: Using what you've learned in this chapter, complete the chart by answering the questions below.

Identity changes with new ideas, experiences, conditions, or in response to other expressions of identity.
What new conditions or identities were African Americans being confronted with during the 1950s?
How did the ideas of the Civil Rights Movement cause Americans as a whole to reexamine or change their own identity? Why?
How did changes in race relations change American identity as a whole?
Why was this change in American identity so difficult for many to accept? Why do you predict changes in American identity took such a long time?
Identity is created, either by a group or person or by outsiders, and self-created identities may be different from how others see one's self.
How did White society view African Americans? What was this perception based on? How were civil rights activists working to change this perception? How did the White-created identity of African Americans shape or explain the different methods or approaches of the Civil Rights Movement?

Handout 5.3: Identity of Civil Rights, continued

Although members of a group/society may have different individual identities, they still share particular elements of identity.
What elements of identity were shared by both races in the 1950s? What different elements of identity appeared in the 1950s? Why?   What did the different racial identities reveal about America in the 1950s?

LESSON 6

Elvis Presley

Alignment of Unit Goals

» Goal 1: To understand the concept of identity in 1950s America.
» Goal 2: To develop skills in historical analysis and song and artwork interpretation.
» Goal 3: To develop analytical and interpretive skills in literature.

Unit Objectives

» To describe how changes in American identity in the 1950s are revealed in the music, art, and literature of the decade;
» To define the context in which a song or piece of art was produced and the implications of context for understanding the artifact;
» To describe a writer's or artist's intent in producing a given song or piece of art based on understanding of text and context;
» To consider short- and long-term consequences of a given document/artifact;
» To describe what a selected literary passage means; and
» To make inferences based on information in given passages.

Resources for Unit Implementation

» **Handout 6.1:** Music Analysis Model

» **Handout 6.2:** Rock 'N Roll in America Identity Chart

» **Listen:** "Every Day I Have the Blues" by B. B. King (1949); "Rocket 88" (Brenston, 1951) by Jackie Brenston and His Delta Cats; "How Many More Years" (Burnett, 1951) by Howlin' Wolf; "Boogie in the Park" by Joe Hill Louis (1949); "Drivin' Slow" by Johnny London (1952); "Bear Cat" by Rufus Thomas (1953); and "Just Walking In The Rain" (Bragg & Riley, 1952) by The Prisonaires. Most songs are available on YouTube.

» **Read:** List of the Top 10 African American musicians of the 1950s from http://www.catalogs.com/info/bestof/top-10-african-american-musicians-in-the-1950s

» **Read:** Excerpts from David Halberstam's (1994) *The Fifties* about radio and music in the 1950s.

» **Listen:** Recordings of Elvis Presley songs: "That's All Right" (Rogers, 1954); "Blue Moon of Kentucky" (Crudup, 1954a); and "I'll Never Let You Go" (Wakeley, 1954). All songs are available on YouTube.

» **Watch:** "Elvis Live 1957" video on YouTube: http://www.youtube.com/watch?v=OFZMCNEf2v8

» **Listen:** Recordings of: Bill Haley and His Comet's "Shake, Rattle, and Roll" (Calhoun, 1955); Chuck Berry's (1955) "Maybellene;" and Little Richard's "Tutti Frutti" (Penniman, 1955). All songs are available on YouTube.

Key Terms

» *Popular culture*: the ideas and attitudes that are in the mainstream of a given culture

Learning Experiences

1. Explain to students that the change in race relations was a slow process, as it required the changing of mindsets and perceptions people had long had of themselves and others. However, other factors helped the process, including popular culture and music. These changes in popular culture and music would not only shape views on race in America, but affect American identity and popular culture as a whole.

2. Give students the Music Analysis Model (Handout 6.1) and have students listen to a song and analyze it: "Every Day I Have the Blues" by B. B. King (1949); "Rocket 88" (Brenston, 1951) by Jackie Brenston and His Delta Cats; "How Many More Years" (Burnett, 1951) by Howlin' Wolf; "Boogie in the Park" by Joe Hill Louis (1949); "Drivin' Slow" by Johnny London (1952); "Bear Cat," by Rufus Thomas (1953); or "Just Walking In The Rain" (Bragg & Riley, 1952) by The Prisonaires. Other songs and artists may be found on the list of the Top 10 musicians of the 1950s mentioned in Resources for Unit Implementation. **Ask:** How does this music compare to the music from Lesson 4? How is the sound different? How are the lyrics different? What is similar? Explain that radio stations were segregated and this music would have been played only on stations that played music by African Americans. This demonstrates the division between the races in the United States in the 1950s.

3. Have students read the excerpts on Elvis from David Halberstam's (1994) *The Fifties* about radio and music in the 1950s. Have the students listen to Elvis Presley's early songs "That's All Right" (Rogers, 1954); "Blue Moon of Kentucky" (Crudup, 1954a); and "I'll Never Let You Go" (Wakeley, 1954). **Ask:** How does Elvis compare to the music we have listened to so far? Which does he sound more like? How does Elvis fulfill the listening preferences of American teenagers described in Halberstam's book?

4. To demonstrate the response to Elvis, watch "Elvis Live 1957" on YouTube. This video also shows his controversial hip shaking. **Ask:** What does it tell us about the 1950s that Elvis became so popular so quickly?

5. Explain that Elvis Presley was not the only artist to cross racial lines in music. Have students listen and analyze Bill Haley and His Comet's "Shake, Rattle, and Roll" (Calhoun, 1955); Chuck Berry's (1955) "Maybellene"; and Little Richard's "Tutti Frutti" (Penniman, 1955) using the Music Analysis Model (Handout 6.1). These songs were all from 1953–1955. **Ask:** What identity is being promoted by these songs— what lifestyle, priorities, values, or concerns? What do these songs suggest about the mood or common culture of America in the mid-1950s?

6. Read the excerpts from Halberstam's (1994) *The Fifties* about teenagers.

7. Have students complete the Rock 'N Roll in America Identity Chart (Handout 6.2). Discuss student responses, first in small groups and then as a large group.

8. Have students go to http://www.elvis.com/about-the-king/music.aspx and look at the number of gold and platinum records and Billboard Top 20 songs he had in his career. **Ask:** What music groups that students listen to today have the same crowd response as the one in the YouTube video? Do they have the same level of production of music?

9. Tell students that Leonard Bernstein, an influential American composer, once said, "Elvis Presley is the greatest cultural force in the 20th century" (Halberstam, 1994, p. 456) and John Lennon said, "Before Elvis, there was nothing" (Halberstam, 1994, p. 457). **Ask:** Why might Bernstein and Lennon have felt this way about Elvis Presley? Do you agree or disagree? Why or why not? How much did you know about Elvis before this lesson? Do you feel Elvis' music still influences American music and culture today? Why or why not? Elvis has been called the King of Rock and Roll. What does this tell us about American culture and the importance of Elvis in American identity?

Assessing Student Learning

» Music Analysis Model
» Rock N' Roll Identity Chart
» Discussions

Extending Student Learning

The following are optional activities for extending student learning in this lesson:

» Have students research rockabilly music, which emerged during the 1950s and was associated with Elvis Presley and other musicians. Have the students share information about the style of music and musicians who performed it.

» Have students locate information about the technology used to record music during the 1950s. Have them compare it to the technology being used now.

» In his recording of "That's All Right" (Crudup, 1954b), Presley melded "Black" and "White" genres in such a way that it was denied airplay on "White" country music radio stations and "Black" R&B stations, dismissed for being defined as both "Black" and "White" music. Have students research how radio stations handled the emergence of music that was barrier-breaking in this way.

Name:_____ Date:_____

HANDOUT 6.1
Music Analysis Model

Directions: Complete the boxes below after listening to the assigned songs.

Song Title:_____

What is the title of the song? Why was it given this title?

Title:
Why do you think it was given this title?
Which words in the title are especially important? Why?

What is your reaction to the song?

What is the first thing about this song that draws your attention?
What is in the song that surprises you, or that you didn't expect?
What are some of the powerful ideas expressed in the song?
What feelings does the song cause in you?
What questions does it raise for you?

Handout 6.1: Music Analysis Model, continued

When was the song written? Why was it written?

Who is the songwriter(s)?	
When was the song written?	
What is the song's purpose? To entertain? To dance to? To critique something?	
What were the important events occurring at the time the song was written?	
Who is the intended audience?	
What biases do you see in the author's lyrics?	

What are the important ideas in this song?

Lyrics	Music/Accompaniment
What is the subject of the song? Summarize the song.	Describe the music or melody of this song. Is it fast-paced or slow? Does it have low notes or high notes? Is it melodic or does it have lots of percussion?
What are the main points of the song? What is the song saying about the subject?	What feelings do you get from the music? Why?
What mood/values/feelings does the singer have about the topic?	How does the tone or mood of the music fit with the lyrics? Why might this be?

What is your evaluation of this song?

What new or different interpretation of this historical period does this song provide?
What does this song portray about American identity or how Americans felt at the time?

Name:_____ Date:_____

HANDOUT 6.2
Rock 'n Roll in America

Directions: Use what you've learned in this chapter to complete the chart by answering the questions below.

Identity changes with new ideas, experiences, conditions, or in response to other expressions of identity.
What new ideas, experiences, or conditions were Americans facing in the mid-1950s? How was this changing American identity? What new characteristics were being introduced? What traits of identity were being altered or lost?
What historical events and changes does Halberstam argue were changing American identity? Do you agree or disagree? Why or why not?
How has the rise of rock-n-roll music shaped American identity to the present?
There are multiple elements of identity and at different times, different elements have greater or lesser importance.
What elements of identity seemed to be more important to people in the mid-1950s? Which elements of identity seemed to be declining in importance? Why was this?

Handout 6.2: Rock 'n Roll in America, continued

Although members of a group or society may have different individual identities, they still share particular elements of identity.
Which segments of American society listened to this music? What traits did they share?

Think about the 1950s America and the trends we have been studying so far in this unit. What can we learn from American teenagers turning to this type of music in large numbers when their parents disagreed with the style?

Are there any traits shared by all Americans revealed in the rise of rock-n-roll music?

LESSON 7

The Beat Generation

Alignment of Unit Goals

» Goal 1: To understand the concept of identity in 1950s America.
» Goal 3: To develop analytical and interpretive skills in literature.
» Goal 4: To develop an understanding of historical events occurring in the United States during the 1950s.

Unit Objectives

» To describe how changes in American identity in the 1950s are revealed in the music, art, and literature of the decade;
» To describe what a selected literary passage means;
» To cite similarities and differences in meaning among selected works of literature;
» To make inferences based on information in given passages; and
» To describe major historical events during the 1950s that affected the American identity.

Resources for Unit Implementation

» **Handout 7.1:** Literature Analysis Model

» **Handout 7.2:** Literature of the Beats

» **Read:** Excerpts from Jack Kerouac's (1957, 1958) books *On the Road* and *The Dharma Bums*.

» **Watch:** Kerouac's readings from YouTube. Footage is available at http://www.youtube.com/watch?v=_MjPtem6ZbE.

» **Read:** Allen Ginsberg's (1955a, 1955b) poems "America" and "Howl." The poems can be found at http://www.poetryarchive.org/poetryarchive/singlePoem.do?poemId=1548 and http://www.poetryfoundation.org/poem/179381. Teachers may want to review Ginsberg's poems for mature content before assigning them to students.

» **Read:** *The New York Times Magazine* article "This Is the Beat Generation" by John Clellon Holmes (1952). The article is available at http://www.litkicks.com/Texts/ThisIsBeatGen.html.

Key Terms

» *The Beats*: a loosely aligned group of friends and writers who emerged during the 1950s and who were known for documenting and inspiring cultural phenomena characterized by the rejection of established standards, innovations in style, and experimentation in various realms

» *Lost Generation*: those people who transitioned from childhood to adulthood during World War I

Learning Experiences

1. Explain to students that during the 1950s, a loosely aligned group of friends and writers emerged that were named "The Beats" by one of their members, Jack Kerouac. Have students read excerpts from Jack Kerouac's (1957, 1958) books *On the Road* and *Dharma Bums* and analyze them using the Literature Analysis Model (Handout 7.1). If possible, listen to Kerouac read his work from YouTube. If you have students listen to his readings, **ask:** What do you notice about how he reads his work?

2. Have students read the two poems by Allen Ginsberg (1955a, 1955b) "America" and "Howl." Have students individually analyze these using the Literature of the Beats sheet (Handout 7.2). Discuss student responses as a whole group. (*Note:* You may also have students analyze the poems using literature analysis models.)

3. **Ask:** How did the Beats feel about American society and the identity that has been constructed in America? Did they dislike America? What were they rebelling against? Why? What traits, figures, and ways of life did they value? What kind of identity were they constructing for themselves? Why might this be? What experiences or events may have led them to these ideas and identity? How does Kerouac compare to Ginsberg? How are they similar? How are they different? What does that tell us about the Beats as a movement?

4. Have students read the *The New York Times Magazine* article "This Is the Beat Generation" by John Clellon Holmes (1952). **Ask:** According to Holmes, what experiences led to the rise of the Beats? What traits define the Beats? What emotions and views do they share?

Holmes compares the Beats to the Lost Generation after World War I. How are the Beats similar to the Lost Generation? In what ways does Holmes stress that the Beats are different from the Lost Generation? How does he describe the overall mood of the Beats? What is the purpose of their quest? Does this mood and motive match what you read from Kerouac? Does Kerouac fit Holmes's description? Why or why not? Does Ginsberg's writing fit Holmes's description? Why or why not?

5. **Ask:** Why was the term "Beat" used? What are the different meanings of "beat"? How do the Beat writers fit these different definitions?

6. **Ask:** How widespread to you think Beat identity was in 1950s America? What do the rise and persistence of the Beats through the decade tell us about the era?

7. Have students write a story of a Beat poet meeting a resident of a Levittown. They should attempt to use the lingo of each group. Have students share their stories in small groups.

Assessing Student Learning

- » Literature Analysis Model
- » Literature of the Beats activity
- » Discussion

Extending Student Learning

The following are optional activities for extending student learning in this lesson:

- » In the reading of Allen Ginsberg's poem "America," students will see a list of people and events that the poet thought were definitive in the shaping of the minds of his generation. Have students brainstorm a list of people and events that they think are definitive of their own generation. They should include these individuals and their works (if possible) in a creative product.
- » A moniker is a name or nickname given to someone for a specific reason. The writers of the 1950s studied in this lesson were given the moniker "The Beat Generation." Have the students develop an appropriate moniker for their own generation and explain the rationale for its use.

Name:_____ Date:_____

HANDOUT 7.1
Literature Analysis Model

Directions: Analyze the excerpts you read by completing the boxes below.

Chosen or assigned text: _____	
Key words:	
Important ideas:	
Tone:	
Mood:	
Imagery:	
Symbolism:	
Structure of writing:	

HANDOUT 7.2

Literature of the Beats

Directions: Answer the questions below.

1. How did the Beats feel about American society and the identity that had been constructed in America?

2. Did they dislike America? What were they rebelling against? Why?

3. What traits, figures, and ways of life did they value? What kind of identity were they constructing for themselves? Why might this be?

4. What experiences or events may have led them to these ideas and identity?

5. How does Kerouac compare to Ginsberg? How are they similar? How are they different? What does that tell us about the Beats as a movement?

LESSON 8

Abstract Expressionism

Alignment of Unit Goals

» Goal 1: To understand the concept of identity in 1950s America.
» Goal 2: To develop skills in historical analysis and song and artwork interpretation.

Unit Objectives

» To describe how changes in American identity in the 1950s are revealed in the music, art, and literature of the decade;
» To define the context in which a song or piece of art was produced and the implications of context for understanding the artifact;
» To describe a writer's or artist's intent in producing a given song/piece of art based on understanding of text and context; and
» To analyze the effects of given documents or artifacts on the interpretation of historical events.

Resources for Unit Implementation

» **Handout 8.1:** Art Analysis Model

» **Handout 8.2:** What Is Abstract Expressionism?

» **View:** Copies of Abstract Expressionist artwork:

○ Willem de Kooning (1950), *Excavation*. Available at http://www.artic.edu/aic/collections/artwork/76244.

○ Willem de Kooning (1955), *Gotham News*. Available at http://www.albrightknox.org/collection/collection-highlights/piece:de-Kooning-gotham-news/.

○ Franz Kline (1950), *Cardinal*. Available at http://www.abstract-art.com/abstraction/l2_grnfthrs_fldr/g035a_kline_cardinal.html.

○ Franz Kline (1959), *Black Reflections*. Available at http://metmuseum.org/toah/works-of-art/64.146.

○ Barnett Newman (1950), *Eve*. Available at http://www.tate.org.uk/art/artworks/newman-eve-t03081.

○ Barnett Newman (1952), *Adam*. Available at http://www.tate.org.uk/art/artworks/newman-adam-t01091.

○ Robert Motherwell (1948–1949), *At Five in the Afternoon*. Available at http://www.artsy.net/artwork/robert-motherwell-at-five-in-the-afternoon.

○ Robert Motherwell (1950), *Mural Fragment*. Available at http://blog.lib.umn.edu/wampr/wamnewsmain/2008/12/growing_pains_a_chronicle_of_r.html.

○ Jackson Pollock (1952), *Blue Poles*. Available at http://nga.gov.au/international/catalogue/Detail.cfm?IRN=36334&MnuID=2&GalID=1.

○ Jackson Pollock (1950), *Autumn Rhythm (Number 30)*. Available at http://www.metmuseum.org/toah/works-of-art/57.92.

» **Watch:** Video of Jackson Pollock at work. Available at http://www.sfmoma.org/explore/multimedia/videos/249

» **Read:** "What Abstract Art Means to Me" by George L. K. Morris, Willem de Kooning, Alexander Calder, Fritz Glarner, Robert Motherwell, and Stuart Davis (1951). A copy of the document is available at http://visualarteducation.wikispaces.com/file/view/Calder_DeKooning_What+Abstract+Art+Means+to+Me.pdf.

Key Terms

» *Abstract Expressionism*: an art movement of the 1940s and 1950s characterized by individual expression and spontaneous creation

Learning Experiences

1. Explain to students that the 1950s gave rise to a new school or group of painters in the United States. In this lesson, students will examine the abstract expressionists.

2. Give students an Art Analysis Model (Handout 8.1). Provide them with copies of paintings or display copies of the artwork from the Internet. Have each student pick one or two images and complete the Art Analysis Model for each painting.

3. **Ask:** What is your reaction to this art? How does this art fit and connect with the traits and experiences of the 1950s in the United States? Is this the type of art you expect to see being made, given what we have been talking about? Why or why not? What is happening in the 1950s that might explain why artists start producing this sort of art?

4. Show students the video of Jackson Pollock at work and explain to students that artists painted on large, wall-sized canvases in many cases. For example, you can see Jackson Pollock is literally standing in his painting. **Ask:** Why might this be? Why such large pieces?

5. Give students the "What Is Abstract Expressionism?" sheet (Handout 8.2) to complete after reading "What Abstract Art Means to Me" (Morris et al., 1951). Discuss student answers.

6. **Ask:** What American values or identity traits are reflected in the Abstract Expressionism movement? What American values or identity traits is the Abstract Expressionism movement rejecting or challenging? Explain that the emphases in Abstract Expressionism were the act of painting, the motions, and the state of being in the painting—how are those emphases a result of the 1950s? What are the artists trying to say?

7. **Ask:** How does the effect of Abstract Expressionism on art compare to the effect of Elvis Presley on music? How does this art reflect American culture of the 1950s? How might this art change American culture? Why?

Assessing Student Learning

» Art Analysis Model activity
» What Is Abstract Expressionism? activity
» Discussion

Extending Student Learning

The following are optional activities for extending student learning in this lesson:

» As Jackson Pollock was becoming famous, many people argued whether his paintings were really "art," or just paint drips on canvas. Have students prepare a rationale for why his paintings could be considered "art."

» Have students research the emergence of photography as a visual art form. Have them hypothesize about how the burgeoning importance of photography related to reactions to works by the abstract expressionists.

Name: _____   Date: _____

HANDOUT 8.1
Art Analysis Model

Directions: Answer the questions below to analyze the art in this chapter.

Artist: _____

Artwork/Image: _____

What is the title of the artwork? Why was it given this title?

Title:
Why do you think it was given this title?
Which words in the title are especially important? Why?
What does the title reveal about the artwork?

What do you see in the artwork?

What objects, shapes, or people do you see?
What colors does the artist use? Why?
Are the images in the work realistic or abstract?
What materials does the artist use? Why?

What is your reaction to the image?

What is the first thing about this image that draws your attention?

Name: _____ Date: _____

What is in the image that surprises you, or that you didn't expect?
What are some of the powerful ideas expressed in the image?
What feelings does the image cause in you?
What questions does it raise for you?

When was the image produced? Why was it produced?

Who is the artist?
When was the artwork produced?
What were the important events occurring at the time the artwork was produced?
What was the author's purpose in producing this artwork?
Who is the intended audience?

What are the important ideas in this artwork?

What assumptions/values/feelings are reflected in the artwork?
What are the artist's views about the issue(s)?

What is your evaluation of this artwork?

What new or different interpretation of this historical period does this artwork provide?
What does this artwork portray about American identity or how Americans felt at the time?

Name:_____ Date: _____

HANDOUT 8.2
What Is Abstract Expressionism?

Directions: Answer the questions below.

1. Read Willem de Kooning's thoughts about art.
   a. What is his view on science and scientists?

   b. Why might this be? Think about the events de Kooning has been through. Why might he feel this way?

   c. How does he view the art his generation is creating? How is this a reaction or response to his feelings about science?

2. Read Robert Motherwell's thoughts on art.
   a. What does he mean that the art is a "fundamentally romantic response to modern life"? What does he feel is wrong with modern life and how does the art seek to address those wrongs?

   b. What is the need he feels? How might events in the world in the 1940s and 1950s have created this need?

LESSON 9

The Day the
Music Died

Alignment of Unit Goals

- » Goal 1: To understand the concept of identity in 1950s America.
- » Goal 2: To develop skills in historical analysis and song and artwork interpretation.
- » Goal 4: To develop an understanding of historical events occurring in the United States during the 1950s.

Unit Objectives

- » To understand the concept of identity in 1950s America;
- » To describe how the American identity changed during the 1950s;
- » To describe how changes in American identity in the 1950s are revealed in the music, art, and literature of the decade;
- » To develop skills in historical analysis and song and artwork interpretation;

> » To define the context in which a song or piece of art was produced and the implications of context for understanding the artifact;
> » To develop an understanding of historical events occurring in the United States during the 1950s; and
> » To describe music, art, and literature of the 1950s that reflected the American identity.

Resources for Unit Implementation

> » **Handout 9.1**: Changes of the 1950s
>
> » **Handout 9.2**: Music Analysis Model
>
> » **Handout 9.3**: Venn Diagram: Music Through the 1950s
>
> » **Listen**: "Peggy Sue" (Holly, Allison, & Petty, 1957) by Buddy Holly; "Come On, Let's Go" (Valens & Keane, 1957) by Ritchie Valens; and "Chantilly Lace" (Foster, Rice, & Richardson, 1958) by The Big Bopper. All songs are available on YouTube.
>
> » **Listen**: "American Pie" by Don McLean (1971). The song is available on YouTube at http://www.youtube.com/watch?v=uAsV5-Hv-7U.

Key Terms

> » *Winter Dance Party*: a tour featuring music stars Buddy Holly, Ritchie Valens, and J. P. "The Big Bopper" Richardson that ended in a fatal plane crash in 1959

Learning Experiences

1. To summarize the decade, have students complete the Changes of the 1950s chart (Handout 9.1) in small groups. Discuss responses as a whole group and **ask:** How is America by the end of the 1950s different from America at the start of the 1950s? Why is this?
2. Explain that during the winter of early 1959, three major music stars, Buddy Holly, Ritchie Valens, and J. P. Richardson (a.k.a. The Big Bopper), were on a tour called the "Winter Dance Party" that ended in a fatal plane crash. These artists were very popular at the time. Have students listen to and analyze the songs of Holly, Valens, and the Big Bopper, using the Music Analysis Model (Handout 9.2).
3. Tell students to think back to the songs they started with in Lesson 4 and the early rock music of Elvis Presley. Have the students complete the Venn Diagram: Music Through the 1950s (Handout 9.3), comparing and contrasting the music from Lesson 4 with the music from this lesson. **Ask:** How are these songs similar? What do the similarities tell us about the U.S. in the 1950s? How are these songs different? How do the differences reflect the changes of the 1950s that we have studied in this unit?
4. Tell students that in 1971, a singer named Don McLean wrote a song about the night Buddy Holly, Ritchie Valens, and the Big Bopper died, which he called "American Pie." Have students listen to and analyze the song. **Ask:** How did McLean view the deaths of these three musicians? How did he describe the world after their death? What does this song tell us about the importance of these musicians of the 1950s? What does this

song tell us about what the music of the 1950s provided to people? How was the world socially, politically, and culturally different after this decade?

5. Have students write a journal as a teenager living in the 1950s. Have them write a diary entry as if it were December 31, 1959, and they are reflecting back on the decade, the things that have happened, and how they feel about them. They also should include their thoughts on the future: What is their outlook for the new decade? What changes do they anticipate, and how do they feel about them? Students should try to stay in the mindset of the 1950s, not today.

Assessing Student Learning

» Changes of the 1950s
» Music Analysis Model
» Venn Diagram: Music Through the 1950s
» Discussion

Extending Student Learning

The following are optional activities for extending student learning in this lesson:

» Have students listen to Billy Joel's (1989) "We Didn't Start the Fire". Have them research the answers to the following questions: Why do you think he chose the particular incidents and people of the 1950s that he did? Is there a pattern in his choices? A message?

» Discuss the causes of teenagers becoming the primary audience for early rock and roll music: they challenged authority, many rock and roll artists were teenagers, the songs reflected their feelings, etc. Have students develop a chronology of rock and roll artists (1950s to today) who could be characterized this way. Have the students describe the similarities and differences in how the musicians expressed their feelings in the past versus today.

Name:_____ Date:_____

HANDOUT 9.1
Changes of the 1950s

Directions: Answer the questions for each category to complete the chart.

How did this change America?	What possibilities did this change present? What positive outcomes might have developed due to this change?	What questions or issues did this change bring to America?
Atomic weapons		
New technology and computers		
McCarthyism and the Red Scare		
The growth of the suburbs		
The start of the Civil Rights Movement		

Name:_____ Date:_____

	What possibilities did this change present? What positive outcomes might have developed due to this change?	What questions or issues did this change bring to America?
How did this change America?		
Elvis Presley and music of the early Civil Rights Movement		
The Beat Generation		
Abstract Expressionism		

Which groups in America were experiencing the most change? (Think racial groups, gender groups, social class, age groups, etc.)

Why were some groups more affected than others? How did this affect American society and identity?

Name:_____ Date: _____

HANDOUT 9.2
Music Analysis Model

Directions: Complete the boxes below after listening to the assigned songs.

Song Title:_____

What is the title of the song? Why was it given this title?

Title:
Why do you think it was given this title?
Which words in the title are especially important? Why?

What is your reaction to the song?

What is the first thing about this song that draws your attention?
What is in the song that surprises you, or that you didn't expect?
What are some of the powerful ideas expressed in the song?
What feelings does the song cause in you?
What questions does it raise for you?

Name:_____ Date: _____

When was the song written? Why was it written?

Who is the songwriter(s)?
When was the song written?
What is the song's purpose? To entertain? To dance to? To critique something?
What were the important events occurring at the time the song was written?
Who is the intended audience?
What biases do you see in the author's lyrics?

What are the important ideas in this song?

Lyrics	Music/Accompaniment
What is the subject of the song? Summarize the song.	Describe the music or melody of this song. Is it fast-paced or slow? Does it have low notes or high notes? Is it melodic or does it have lots of percussion?
What are the main points of the song? What is the song saying about the subject?	What feelings do you get from the music? Why?
What mood/values/feelings does the singer have about the topic?	How does the tone or mood of the music fit with the lyrics? Why might this be?

What is your evaluation of this song?

What new or different interpretation of this historical period does this song provide?
What does this song portray about American identity or how Americans felt at the time?

HANDOUT 9.3

Venn Diagram:
Music Through the 1950s

Directions: Compare and contrast the music from Lesson 4 to the music you listened to in this lesson and complete the Venn diagram below.

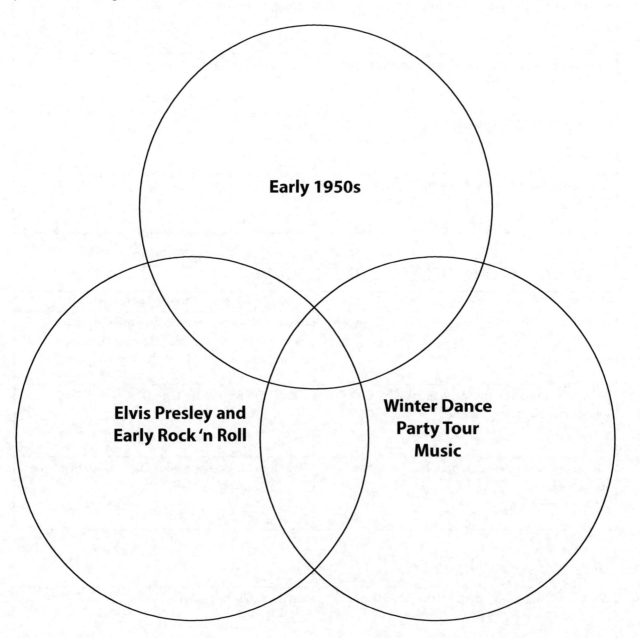

LESSON 10

Evaluating the 1950s

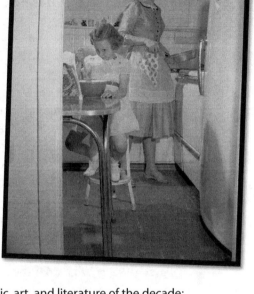

Alignment of Unit Goals

» Goal 1: To understand the concept of identity in 1950s America.
» Goal 4: To develop an understanding of historical events occurring in the United States during the 1950s.

Unit Objectives

» To understand the concept of identity in 1950s America;
» To describe how the American identity changed during the 1950s;
» To describe how changes in American identity in the 1950s are revealed in the music, art, and literature of the decade;
» To develop an understanding of historical events occurring in the United States during the 1950s;
» To describe major historical events during the 1950s that affected the American identity; and
» To describe music, art, and literature of the 1950s that reflected the American identity.

Resources for Unit Implementation

» **Handout 10.1:** Venn Diagram: TV Versus Reality
» **Handout 10.2:** American Identity in the 1950s
» **Watch:** Clips of *Leave It to Beaver*, *Father Knows Best*, and/or *The Adventures of Ozzie & Harriet*. A variety of clips from each show is available on YouTube.

Key Terms

» *Popular culture*: the ideas and attitudes that are in the mainstream of a given culture
» *Identity*: the characteristics by which a person or thing is recognized

Learning Experiences

1. Have students present their *The Ed Sullivan Show* schedules and explain their choices. Discuss as a whole group what the student-created shows have in common and how they differ. **Ask:** How would you describe America in the 1950s based on your research?

2. Watch clips from *Leave It to Beaver*, *Father Knows Best*, and/or *The Adventures of Ozzie & Harriet*. Based on the clips, have students list the traits of the father, mother, and the children portrayed. **Ask:** Looking at the list of traits and characteristics, does this match your view of America in the 1950s? Why or why not?

3. Have students complete the Venn Diagram: TV Versus Reality (Handout 10.1). **Ask:** How were the 1950s presented in popular culture and the 1950s in reality similar and how were they different? Why did TV create this identity for American people despite the reality? What does it tell us about identity in America in the 1950s? These shows were popular and continue to be—why is this so? What does the popularity of this constructed American identity tell us about actual American identity? What do we value and how do we want to perceive ourselves?

4. Ask students to think about TV shows today. In small groups, have students list popular TV shows and how they portray American families and the American identity. **Ask:** How does the portrayal of families on TV today compare to how families were portrayed on TV in the 1950s? What does the difference in TV families in the 1950s and today tell us about how our country has changed over time? Do TV shows today match the reality of our experiences? In what ways? Why not? What does the portrayal of families on TV tell us about American identity today?

5. Have students complete the American Identity in the 1950s chart (Handout 10.2) in small groups or individually. Discuss student responses as a whole group. Have students take out the Identity Charts they started with in Lesson 1. **Ask:** How has it changed? Has it changed more than you expected or less? Why? What experiences or conditions most changed American identity over the decade? What elements of identity seemed to be the most important at the end of the decade? Why? What different identities still exist that are creating tension in the United States?

6. Explain to students that they will see how these changes continue in the 1960s.

Assessing Student Learning

» Formative assessment: *The Ed Sullivan Show* schedules
» Venn diagram activity
» Formative assessment: American Identity in the 1950s activity

Extending Student Learning

The following are optional activities for extending student learning in this lesson:

» Have students interview someone who was of middle school age (the students' age) during the 1950s. The students should pose questions about what is the same and different in pop culture for teenagers then and now.

» Have students view excerpts of three movies of the era that feature rebellious youth: *Rebel Without a Cause*, *The Wild One*, and *Blackboard Jungle*. Clips and the trailers from each film are on YouTube. Have students develop a description about how life has or has not changed in the time since the movies were first viewed.

HANDOUT 10.1

Venn Diagram:
TV Versus Reality

Directions: Use the clips you've watched to complete the Venn diagram below.

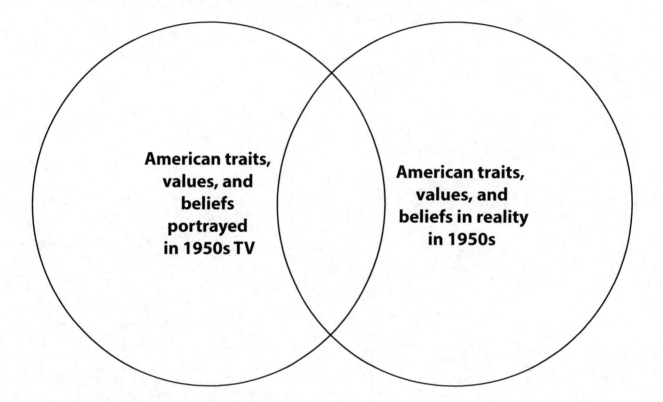

American traits, values, and beliefs portrayed in 1950s TV

American traits, values, and beliefs in reality in 1950s

HANDOUT 10.2

American Identity
in the 1950s

Directions: Use what you've learned in this unit to define American identity at the end of the 1950s by completing the chart below.

Identity	Time and Place
	Culture and Traditions
	History and Myths
	International Role
	Economy
	Civic Identity
	Race/Ethnicity

Name:_____ Date: _____

1. *Race and ethnicity:* How did views on race changed through the 1950s? How did changing racial roles change American identity?

2. *Culture and traditions:* What new traditions or cultural traits emerged in the U.S. during the 1950s? How did this change American values and identity?

3. *History and myths:* What historical events shaped the mindset of the 1950s? What myths were created or held by Americans in the 1950s?

4. *Economy:* What was the state of the U.S. economy in 1959 compared to 1950? What changed? How did this change American culture and values and identity?

5. *International role:* How did America's international role in the 1950s shape life in the U.S. during this decade?

6. *Time and Place/ Civic Identity:* How would you describe the effects of the events of the 1950s on the U.S.? How did the 1950s create or shape the America we live in today?

References

Asimov, I. (1953a). Franchise. In *Earth is room enough*. New York, NY: Quinn.

Asimov, I. (1953b). Nobody here but . . . . In F. Pohl (Ed.), *Star science fiction stories*. New York, NY: Ballantine.

Asimov, I. (1955). Youth. In *The Martian way and other stories*. New York, NY: Doubleday.

Bagdasarian, R., & Saroyan, W. (1951). Come on-a my house [Recorded by Rosemary Clooney]. On *Come on-a my house* [Record]. New York, NY: Columbia.

Beals, M. P. (2001). *Warriors don't cry: A searing memoir of the battle to integrate Little Rock's Central High*. New York, NY: Simon Pulse.

Benjamin, B., & Weiss, G. D. (1951). Wheel of fortune [Recorded by Kay Starr]. On *Wheel of fortune* [Record]. New York, NY: Capitol.

Berry, C. (1955). Maybellene. On *Maybellene* [Record]. New York, NY: Chess.

Bradbury, R. (1950). There will come soft rains. In *The Martian Chronicles*. New York, NY: Doubleday.

Bradbury, R. (1951a). The concrete mixer. In *The illustrated man*. New York, NY: Doubleday.

Bradbury, R. (1951b). Zero hour. In *The illustrated man*. New York, NY: Doubleday.

Bradbury, R. (1953). *Fahrenheit 451*. New York, NY: Ballantine.

Bragg, J., & Riley, R. (1952). Just walkin' in the rain [Recorded by The Prisonaires]. On *Just walkin' in the rain* [Record]. New York, NY: Sun Records.

Brenston, J. (1951). Rocket 88 [Recorded by Jackie Brenston and His Delta Cats]. On *Jackie Brenston and His Delta Cats* [Record]. New York, NY: Chess.

Burnett, C. (1951). How many more years [Recorded by Howlin' Wolf]. On *Moanin' in the moonlight* [Record]. New York, NY: Chess.

Calhoun, C. E. (1955). Shake, rattle, and roll [Recorded by Bill Haley and His Comets]. On *Shake, rattle, and roll* [Record]. New York, NY: Decca Records.

Center for Gifted Education. (2007). *Guide to teaching social studies curriculum*. Dubuque, IA: Kendall Hunt.

Center for Gifted Education. (2011). *Autobiographies and memoirs*. Dubuque, IA: Kendall Hunt.

Clarke, A. C. (1953). If I forget thee, oh Earth. In A. Clarke (Ed.), *Expedition to Earth*. New York, NY: Ballantine.

Cole, N. K. (2009). We are Americans too [Recorded by Nat King Cole]. On *Voices of change, then and now* [CD]. New York, NY: Capitol USA. (1956)

Crudup, A. (1954a). Blue moon of Kentucky [Recorded by Elvis Presley]. On *Blue moon of Kentucky* [Record]. Memphis, TN: Sun.

Crudup, A. (1954b). That's all right [Recorded by Elvis Presley]. On *Blue moon of Kentucky* [Record]. Memphis, TN: Sun.

de Kooning, W. (1950). *Excavation* [Painting]. Retrieved from http://www.artic.edu/aic/collections/artwork/76244

de Kooning, W. (1955). *Gotham news* [Painting]. Retrieved from http://www.albrightknox.org/collection/collection-highlights/piece:de-Kooning-gotham-news

Doll, J. (1951). When they drop the atomic bomb [Recorded by Jackie Doll and His Pickled Peppers]. On *When they drop the atomic bomb* [Record]. Chicago, IL: Mercury.

Eisenhower, D. D. (1953, June). *Don't join the book burners.* Speech presented at the Dartmouth College Commencement, Hanover, NH. Retrieved from http://www.presidency.ucsb.edu/ws/?pid=9606

Ellison, R. (1952). *Invisible man.* New York, NY: Random House.

Fain, S. (1938). I can dream, can't I? [Recorded by The Andrews Sisters]. On *I can dream, can't I?* [Record]. New York, NY: Decca. (1949)

Foster, J., Rice, B., & Richardson, J. P. (1958). Chantilly lace. On *Chantilly lace* [Record]. Chicago, IL: Mercury.

Ginsberg, A. (1955a). America. In *Howl and other poems.* San Francisco, CA: City Lights Books.

Ginsberg, A. (1955b). Howl. In *Howl and other poems.* San Francisco, CA: City Lights Books.

Golden Gate Quartet. (1947). Atom and evil. On *Atom and evil* [Record]. New York, NY: Columbia.

Green, R. L. (2010). *The adventures of Robin Hood.* London, England: Puffin.

Hales, P. B. (2013). *Levittown: Documents of an ideal American suburb.* Retrieved from http://tigger.uic.edu/~pbhales/Levittown

Halberstam, D. (1994). *The fifties.* New York, NY: Ballantine.

Hamilton, N., & Lewis, M. (1940). How high the moon [Recorded by Les Paul]. On *How high the moon* [Record]. New York, NY: Capitol. (1951)

Hammerstein, A., & Wilkinson, D. (1940). Because of you [Recorded by Tony Bennett]. On *Because of you* [Record]. New York, NY: Columbia.

Holly, B., Allison, J., & Norman, P. (1957). Peggy Sue. On *Buddy Holly* [Record]. New York, NY: Coral.

Holmes, J. C. (1952, November). This is the Beat generation. *New York Times Magazine.* Retrieved from http://www.litkicks.com/Texts/ThisIsBeatGen.html

Hughes, L. (1990). Harlem. In *Selected Poems of Langston Hughes.* New York, NY: Random House. (Original work published in 1951)

Huntington, S. P. (2004). *Who are we? The challenges to America's national identity.* New York, NY: Simon and Schuster.

Joel, B. (1989). We didn't start the fire. On *Storm front* [Record]. New York, NY: Columbia.

Kerouac, J. (1957). *On the road.* New York, NY: Viking Press.

Kerouac, J. (1958). *The dharma bums.* New York, NY: Viking Press.

King, B. B. (1949). Every day I have the blues [Recorded by B. B. King]. On *Singin the blues* [Record]. New York, NY: RPM/Kent.

Kline, F. (1950). *Cardinal* [Painting]. Retrieved from http://www.abstract-art.com/abstraction/12_grnfthrs_fldr/g035a_kline_cardinal.html

Kline, F. (1959). *Black reflections* [Painting]. Retrieved from http://metmuseum.org/toah/works-of-art/64.146

Ledbetter, H. (1934). Goodnight Irene [Recorded by The Weavers]. On *Goodnight Irene* [Record]. New York, NY: Decca. (1950)

Library of Congress. (n.d.). *Using primary sources.* Retrieved from http://www.loc.gov/teachers/usingprimarysources/

London, J. (1952). Drivin' slow. On *Drivin' slow* [Record]. New York, NY: Sun Records.

Louis, J. H. (1949). Boogie in the park. On *Boogie in the park* [Record]. New York, NY: Sun Records.

Louvin, I., Louvin, C., & Bain, B. (1952). Great atomic power [Recorded by The Louvin Brothers]. On *The Louvin Brothers* [Record]. New York, NY: MGM.

McCarthy, J. (1950, February). *Enemies from within*. Lincoln Day speech presented to Republican Women's Club in Wheeling, WV. Retrieved from http://historymatters.gmu.edu/d/6456

McKeague, P. M. (2009). *Writing about literature* (9th ed.). Dubuque, IA: Kendall Hunt.

McLean, D. (1971). American pie. On *American pie* [Record]. New York, NY: United Artists.

Morris, G. L. K., de Kooning, W., Calder, A., Glarner, F., Motherwell, R., & Davis, S. (1951). What abstract art means to me. *The Bulletin of the Museum of Modern Art, 18*(3), 2–15.

Motherwell, R. (1948–1949). *At five in the afternoon* [Painting]. Retrieved from http://www.artsy.net/artwork/robert-motherwell-at-five-in-the-afternoon

Motherwell, R. (1950). *Mural fragment* [Painting]. Retrieved from http://blog.lib.umn.edu/wampr/wamnewsmain12008?121growing_pains_a_chronicle_of_r.html

National Governors Association Center for Best Practices, & Council of Chief State School Officers. (2010). *Common Core State Standards for English language arts and literacy in history/social studies, science, and technical subjects*. Washington, DC: Authors.

Newman, B. (1950). *Eve* [Painting]. Retrieved from http://www.tate.org.uk/art/artworks/newman-eve-t03081

Newman, B. (1952). *Adam* [Painting]. Retrieved from http://www.tate.org.uk/art/artworks/newman-adam-t01091

Orwell, G. (1949). *1984*. London, England: Secker and Warburg.

Partlow, V. (1950). Old man atom [Recorded by The Sons of the Pioneers]. On *Old man atom* [Record]. New York, NY: RCA Victor.

Penniman, L. R. (1955). Tutti frutti [Recorded by Little Richard]. On *Here's Little Richard* [Record]. New York, NY: Specialty Records.

Pollock, J. (1948). *Number 4* [Painting]. Retrived from http://www.wikipaintings.org/en/jackson-pollock/number-4-gray-and-red-1948

Pollock, J. (1950). *Autumn rhythm (Number 30)* [Painting]. Retrieved from http://www.metmuseum.org/toah/works-of-art/57.92

Pollock, J. (1952). *Blue poles* [Painting]. Retrieved from http://nga.gov.au/international/catalogue/Detail.cfm?IRN=36334&MnuID=2&GalID=1

Rogers, J. (1954). That's all right [Recorded by Elvis Presley]. On *That's all right* [Record]. New York, NY: RCA Victor.

Rolfe, E. (1953a). Ballad of the noble intentions. In C., Nelson & J. Hendricks (Eds.), *Edwin Rolfe: Collected poems* (pp. 224–226). Chicago: University of Illinois Press.

Rolfe, E. (1953b). Little ballad for Americans. In C., Nelson & J. Hendricks (Eds.), *Edwin Rolfe: Collected poems* (pp. 224–226). Chicago: University of Illinois Press.

Rolfe, E. (1953c). Political prisoner 123456789. In C., Nelson & J. Hendricks (Eds.), *Edwin Rolfe: Collected poems* (pp. 224–226). Chicago: University of Illinois Press.

Seeger, P. (1955). Wasn't that a time [Recorded by The Weavers]. On *Wasn't that a time* [Record]. New York, NY: Vanguard.

Smith, A. D. (2010). *National identity (Ethnonationalism comparative perspective)*. Malden, MA: Polity Press.

Taba, H. (1962). *Curriculum development: Theory and practice*. New York, NY: Harcourt Brace World.

Thomas, R. (1953). Bear cat. On *Bear cat* [Record]. New York, NY: Sun Records.

Thoreau, H. D. (1849). Civil disobedience. In E. Peabody (Ed.), *Aesthetic papers*. New York, NY: G. P. Putnam.

United States Federal Civil Defense Administration. (Producer). (1951). *Duck and cover: Bert the turtle civil defense film* [Motion picture]. Nashville, TN: Archer Productions.

Valens, R., & Keane, B. (1957). Come on, let's go. On *Ritchie Valens* [Record]. Los Angeles, CA: Del-Fi.

Wakeley, J. (1954). I'll never let you go [Recorded by Elvis Presley]. On *Elvis Presley* [Record]. New York, NY: RCA Victor.

Weinman, B., & Dorney, R. (1954). Get that Communist, Joe [Recorded by The Kavaliers]. On *Get that communist, Joe* [Record]. New York, NY: Republic.

Wilson, S. (1955). *The man in the gray flannel suit.* Cambridge, MA: Da Capo Press.

APPENDIX A

Unit Glossary

Abstract Expressionism: an art movement of the 1940s and 1950s characterized by individual expression and spontaneous creation

The Beats: a loosely aligned group of friends and writers who emerged during the 1950s and who were known for documenting and inspiring cultural phenomena characterized by the rejection of established standards, innovations in style, and experimentation in various realms

civil rights: rights that protect one's individual freedoms within a society

conformity: matching one's behaviors and attitudes to the group's norms

identity: the characteristics by which a person or thing is recognized

Levittown: suburban developments in which identical homes were produced for returning veterans and first-time homebuyers

Lost Generation: those people who transitioned from childhood to adulthood during World War I

McCarthyism: making accusations of disloyalty or subversion without evidence. The term was named after U.S. Senator Joseph McCarthy of Wisconsin because of his anti-Communist concerns

popular culture: the ideas and attitudes that are in the mainstream of a given culture

Red Scare: the concern about the rise of Communism

science fiction: a genre of fiction dealing with future settings and imagined content

soda fountain: a machine that dispenses carbonated soft drinks; soda fountains located in pharmacies and ice cream parlors became public places where people could socialize

suburb: a residential area outside a city

technology: any new tool developed to solve a problem

Winter Dance Party: a tour featuring music stars Buddy Holly, Ritchie Valens, and J. P. "The Big Bopper" Richardson that ended in a fatal plane crash in 1959

Teacher's Guide to Art Content

(For use with Lesson 8)

The Abstract Expressionist movement began in the 1940s and continued into the 1950s. Following WWII, New York City became, for the very first time, the nexus of the art world. Up until then, for more than 200 years, Paris had been the center of the art stage. The crisis that came with the war and its aftermath is key to understanding this art movement. Prior to and during WWII, several leading artists, many of them Surrealists, living in Europe fled to the U.S., particularly to New York City. American artists were themselves concerned with the dark side of human nature and anxious about the future. The influx of European artists influenced the American artists in style and helped foster an interest in the unconscious. Myth and archetypal symbols also helped shape the concept of painting itself as a struggle between conscious and unconscious expression. This new mix of New York painters, inspired by the Surrealists and Abstractionists, wanted to create an innovative movement that reflected the stress and anxiety following the war. They wanted to express profound emotion in their painting and illustrate universal themes (Beckett, 1994).

This new movement came to be called *Abstract Expressionism*. Abstract Expressionism really was not about a specific style but more about an attitude or belief (Janson & Janson, 2001). It was a rebellion against Social Realism and Regionalism, both figurative painting styles that were prevalent in the 1920s and 1930s. Many of the American Social Realist and Regionalist artists had experienced the Great Depression, and several had worked in the Social Realism style as young artists, often as part of the the Works Progress Administration (WPA), a New Deal agency that employed musicians and artists in large-scale art projects. By the late 1940s, most artists had abandoned these styles but kept a hold on the monumental scale of the murals that they had painted for the WPA. These artists did not feel that any conventional subject and style could adequately express their new vision or express what was happening in the country and the world.

Abstract Expressionism was a break from the past and was stylistically very diverse. The artists valued spontaneity and improvisation. The movement can be roughly divided into two basic categories, although even this is challenging because of the individualistic nature of each artist's work. The first category is "action painting," which consisted of paintings done with large, expressive, and dynamic movements. The second category is "color field painting," which dealt with the expressive nature of color; simplified, sometimes to the point of being an entire canvas of a single color, these paintings had a large, color-dominated field. These two styles were connected by abstract imagery. For Abstract Expressionists, the value of the art was in individual expression and spontaneous creation. The artwork was meant to be a revelation of the artist's identity. Paintings were meant to be seen in relatively close quarters so the monumental scale created a sense of being engulfed by the work (Janson & Janson, 2001).

Artists of the "action painting" school often worked on very large canvases on the floor, on or around which they would walk using big, expressive movements to apply the paint (Gombrich, 1995). Perhaps the most famous of these artists is Jackson Pollack, who dripped, splattered, and poured multiple layers of paint to create complex, layered images. He invented a new technique by using no tools, brushes, stretchers, or easels to create something entirely subjective on a huge scale. In the "color field painting" school, Mark Rothko was one of the leading artists and created large, very simple paintings of color. Willem de Kooning, Franz Kline, and Robert Motherwell are just a few of the other important Abstract Expressionists. By the end of the 1950s, Abstract Expressionism had mostly lost its place as the forefront of the art world, replaced by Pop Art. However, it is still a vital reflection of the 1950s in America.

References

Beckett, W. (1994). *Sister Wendy's story of painting*. New York, NY: DK Pub.

Gombrich, E. H. (1995). *The story of art* (16th ed.). London, England: Phaidon Press.

Janson, H. W., & Janson, A. F. (2001). *History of art* (6th ed.). New York, NY: Harry N. Abrams.

 About the Authors

Molly Sandling is a teacher at Jamestown High School in Williamsburg, VA, where she teaches AP U.S. History and AP Human Geography. She completed her master's degree in history at Yale University and her master's degree in education at the College of William & Mary, with an emphasis on adolescent social studies education. While in the master's degree program, she wrote the social studies units *The 1920s in America: A Decade of Tensions, The 1930s in America: Facing Depression, Defining Nations,* and *The Renaissance and Reformation in Europe* and received the NAGC Curriculum Award for *The 1920s in America*. Molly has been teaching since 2000 and was the 2010 High School Teacher of the Year for Williamsburg-James City County Public Schools.

Kimberley Chandler, Ph.D., is the Curriculum Director at the Center for Gifted Education at the College of William and Mary and a clinical assistant professor. Kimberley completed her Ph.D. in Educational Policy, Planning, and Leadership with an emphasis in gifted education administration at the College of William and Mary. Her professional background includes teaching gifted students in a variety of settings, serving as an administrator of a school district gifted program, and providing professional development training for teachers and administrators nationally and internationally. Currently, Kimberley is the Network Representative on the NAGC Board of Directors, Member-at-Large Representative for the AERA Research on Giftedness and Talent SIG, and editor of the CEC-TAG newsletter *The Update*. Her research interests include curriculum policy and implementation issues in gifted programs, the design and evaluation of professional development programs for teachers of the gifted, and the role of principals in gifted education. Kimberley coauthored a book titled *Effective Curriculum for Underserved Gifted Students* and has served as the editor of many curriculum materials (science, social studies, language arts, and mathematics) from the Center for Gifted Education at The College of William and Mary.

Common Core State Standards Alignment

Grade Levels	Common Core State Standards in ELA-Literacy
K-12 College and Career Readiness Anchor Standards	L.CCRA.R.1: Read closely to determine what the text says explicitly and to make logical inferences from it; cite specific textual evidence when writing or speaking to support conclusions drawn from the text.
	L.CCRA.R.2: Determine central ideas or themes of a text and analyze their development; summarize the key supporting details and ideas.
	L.CCRA.R.4: Interpret words and phrases as they are used in a text, including determining technical, connotative, and figurative meanings, and analyze how specific word choices shape meaning or tone.
	L.CCRA.R.7: Integrate and evaluate content presented in diverse media and formats, including visually and quantitatively, as well as in words.
	L.CCRA.R.9: Analyze how two or more texts address similar themes or topics in order to build knowledge or to compare the approaches the authors take.
	L.CCRA.R.10: Read and comprehend complex literary and informational texts independently and proficiently.